"*The Business of Human Rights* provides both a powerful argument for why businesses should take on the protection of human rights and a thoroughly practical guide book to how they can do so. It should be on the required reading list of every human rights activist and every corporate executive."

Michael W. Doyle, Columbia University, former UN Assistant Secretary-General for Policy Planning and Special Adviser to SG Kofi Annan

"The old business mantra that human rights are matters for politicians is even less valid in today's world of full transparency and media- and social media-intrusive scrutiny than it ever was. Corporate reputations can stand or fall on their treatment of human rights – see the hugely costly damage to the bottom lines of those global corporates complicit in ex-South African President Zuma's corruption. I strongly recommend Alex Newton's *The Business of Human Rights* as a straight-forward and engaging guide for business executives, public officials and students."

Lord Peter Hain, Former British Cabinet Minister and Member of Parliament

The Business of Human Rights

The spotlight of global scrutiny has shone particularly brightly on corporations' adverse impacts on human rights in recent years. Corporations make up more than two-thirds of the world's top economies today, and so rightly they are being called to account for their impacts on society and the communities in which they operate. *The Business of Human Rights* demystifies the relevance of human rights for business, explaining how the corporate responsibility to respect human rights under the UN Guiding Principles can be implemented in practice. It provides a straightforward, practical guide that can be easily read and interpreted by managers to help businesses navigate this complex area of legislation and "soft" law to fulfil their responsibilities. It explains the potential legal, financial and reputational implications for corporations and the steps they need to take to address them.

The book tracks some of the major global developments in business and human rights, including the emergence of foreign, transnational, and international law and the proliferation of multi-stakeholder initiatives on business and human rights. Case studies from a range of sectors and industries – such as extractives, apparel, fast-moving consumer goods, electronics, and banking and finance – illustrate the enormous risks and opportunities human rights pose for business in practice.

The Business of Human Rights will equip corporate executives, sustainability practitioners, academics, students, and anyone interested in business's impacts on society with the essential information and tools they need to quickly come up to speed with the rapidly evolving area of business and human rights.

Alex Newton is a lawyer and specialist in responsible business and human rights. Her consultancy advises corporations, governments, and non-governmental organisations on a wide range of matters related to business and human rights, anti-discrimination, reputation risk, and governance. She regularly writes and speaks on these topics in Australia and internationally.

The Business of Human Rights

Best Practice and the UN Guiding Principles

Alex Newton

Routledge
Taylor & Francis Group

LONDON AND NEW YORK

First published 2019
by Routledge
2 Park Square, Milton Park, Abingdon, Oxon OX14 4RN

and by Routledge
52 Vanderbilt Avenue, New York, NY 10017

Routledge is an imprint of the Taylor & Francis Group, an informa business

British Library Cataloguing-in-Publication Data
A catalogue record for this book is available from the British
Library

Library of Congress Cataloging-in-Publication Data
Names: Newton, Alex, 1979– author.
Title: The business of human rights : best practice and the UN
guiding principles / Alex Newton.
Description: 1 Edition. | New York : Routledge, 2019. |
Includes bibliographical references and index. |
Identifiers: LCCN 2018058366 (print) | LCCN 2019004044
(ebook) | ISBN 9781351131193 (978-1-351-13119-3) |
ISBN 9781783538218 (hardback : alk. paper) |
ISBN 9781783537150 (pbk. : alk. paper) |
ISBN 9781351131193 (ebk)
Subjects: LCSH: Social responsibility of business. | Human
rights. | United Nations. Human Rights Council.
Classification: LCC HD60 (ebook) | LCC HD60 .N478 2019
(print) | DDC 658.4/08–dc23
LC record available at https://lccn.loc.gov/2018058366

ISBN: 978-1-78353-821-8 (hbk)
ISBN: 978-1-78353-715-0 (pbk)
ISBN: 978-1-351-13119-3 (ebk)

Typeset in Sabon
by Wearset Ltd, Boldon, Tyne and Wear

For Anneliese

Contents

Illustrations

Figure

Tables

Acknowledgements

I am very grateful to many people who have supported me along the journey of taking this book from concept to reality.

To my editor, Rebecca Marsh, at Taylor and Francis (Routledge): thank you for all your encouragement, feedback and assistance throughout the process. It has been a great pleasure working with you.

Huge thanks also to Michael W. Doyle and Anthony Ewing at Columbia University, for reviewing and commenting on the draft manuscript. I have learned so much from both of you over the years, and very much appreciate your invaluable advice and insights.

To my family: many thanks to Tony Newton for reading the manuscript and for your constructive suggestions to improve it. And to Grandmas Wendy and Susan, and Grandpa Seri: thank you very much for many hours of babysitting, which gave me the time to write.

To Anneliese: thank you for being the loveliest baby I could ever have wished for, and for not minding that your mum had a book to write.

Finally, thank you so much to Eddy Thientosapol, my partner and best friend, for being an incredible person and for supporting me in everything.

About the author

Alex Newton is a lawyer and specialist in business and human rights. She consults to corporations, governments and non-governmental organisations on a wide range of matters relating to responsible business, human rights, anti-discrimination, public policy, and governance.

Before launching her consulting business, she worked as a Director and Executive in Australia's Department of the Prime Minister and Cabinet, advising on complex legal and public policy issues. Previously, she served in the United Nations Secretary-General's Strategic Planning Unit in New York and as a lawyer with the Australian Human Rights Commission. She started her career as a commercial lawyer with King and Wood Mallesons.

Newton established the business and human rights course in the Australian National University's postgraduate law programme and lectured there from 2010 until 2015. She has also lectured in international human rights law at the University of Technology, Sydney.

She is a member of the GEC Risk Advisory Team, a New York-based consulting firm specialising in governance and reputation risk management.

She lives in Sydney, Australia, with her family.

How this book came about

As an advisor to corporations and governments on responsible business and human rights, I find my work often prompts quizzical expressions and sometimes even looks of bewilderment from corporate executives. They ask:

- *What does business have to do with human rights?*
- *Isn't it government's role to address human rights issues?*
- *Surely only poor countries have these problems?*
- *We're a good company. We never abuse human rights! How could this apply to us?*
- *Our company didn't intend to impact human rights, so surely it can't be held responsible, can it?*

To some extent, this confusion is understandable. For many years the public and private spheres remained largely distinct, and responsibility for human rights fell squarely (and uniquely) within the domain of nation States, not private actors.

However, in the twenty-first century, this is no longer the case. Corporations now make up more than two-thirds of the world's top economies. With the increasing power of corporations has come a growing awareness of their potential impacts – both positive and negative – not only on their employees and stakeholders, but also on the communities in which they operate.

Tragically, there are many examples of corporations involved in human rights abuses across different industries and in many countries. The 2013 Rana Plaza factory collapse in Bangladesh killed 1,135 garment workers, maimed hundreds more, and implicated many global fashion brands in the process. A slew of worker suicides at Apple's Chinese manufacturer, Foxconn, shone the spotlight of public scrutiny on the technology giant and its supply chain. The catastrophic collapse of Samarco's tailings dam in Bento Rodrigues, Brazil, caused loss of life, the destruction of an entire community's homes and livelihoods, and irreparable environmental damage. Joint venture partners Vale and BHP Billiton were also called to account for their role in the tragedy.

Sadly, the list goes on. One only needs to turn on the television or open a newspaper to find more examples of adverse impacts on human rights linked to corporate action or inaction. While previously many of these cases may have slipped under the public's radar, the modern 24-hour news cycle and the ubiquity of social media now means that accountability has never been greater.

This book seeks to answer the questions posed above and to offer some clarity amid the confusion. It aims to provide a straightforward introduction to the business and human rights field for the busy corporate executive, public official, practitioner, or student. While it certainly cannot hope to touch on every area in this rapidly expanding (and constantly changing) field, it will provide an introductory primer that will equip the reader with the key essentials they need to understand the corporate responsibility to respect human rights and what it means for business.

Part I

Introduction

Chapter 1

What is business and human rights?

Human rights

Before we address the topic of business and human rights, it is necessary to take a step back to first consider the concept of human rights itself.

While the term "human rights" is frequently bandied about in daily discourse, its content and meaning are not always fully understood. In essence, human rights are the universal rights and freedoms that apply to everyone, irrespective of their gender, race, religion, or country of origin. They aim to secure dignity and equality for all people.

At the international level, human rights are enshrined in international treaties. At the national level, many countries have implemented their international human rights obligations in domestic legislation. For other countries, their international obligations are "automatically" incorporated in their domestic law when they sign and ratify an international treaty.

The 1948 *Universal Declaration of Human Rights* ("UDHR") is considered the cornerstone of the international human rights system. It was drafted in the aftermath of the Second World War to prevent a recurrence of the atrocities in the war.

The UDHR recognises all the main human rights, including civil and political rights (like the rights to life, to free speech, to a fair trial, and to freedom from torture and slavery) and economic and social rights (such as the rights to health, to social security, to education, to a fair wage, and to favourable working conditions).

The UDHR was codified into international law through two 1966 treaties: the *International Covenant on Civil and Political Rights* ("ICCPR")[1] and the *International Covenant on Economic, Social and Cultural Rights* ("ICESCR").[2] Together, these three documents form the *International Bill of Rights*. We underline its importance from the outset and will return to it throughout this book.

Aside from the *International Bill of Rights*, there are various treaties that are notable for specifically addressing the rights of certain groups of people. Among others, these include: women (*Convention on the Elimination of All Forms of Discrimination Against Women*), people with disabilities (*Convention on the Rights of Persons with Disabilities*), children (*Convention on the Rights of the Child*), and refugees (*Convention Relating to the Status of Refugees*).

Since it was established, the international human rights law framework has principally governed nation States, not individuals or corporate actors. Under the framework, States have obligations to respect, protect, promote and fulfil human rights. (An exception to this is the obligations that corporations and individuals owe under international criminal law. This will be discussed further in Chapter 6.)

In turn, it has been the role of nation States to regulate corporate actors' behaviour within their territory or jurisdiction to the extent that it impacts detrimentally on human rights. States meet these obligations in a range of ways, including by enacting and enforcing domestic legislation, providing judicial remedies, and imposing regulations and reporting requirements on business.

This division between States' and corporations' responsibilities works well in theory. However, it has often broken down in practice as the tentacles of transnational corporations' supply chains have spread out further and further, entangling many more suppliers and contractors in far-flung places, and across multiple jurisdictions, in their path. Gaps have emerged where no

State is either willing or able to regulate corporations' behaviour when it comes to human rights.

These "gaps" in governance between the international and national human rights law systems when it comes to governing corporate conduct underpin the genesis of the business and human rights movement.

Business and human rights

As global supply chains have become increasingly complex and attenuated, and as corporations have entered more and more emerging markets, transitional democracies, and those in conflict or post-conflict situations, the deficiencies of many States' abilities to regulate the human rights impacts of business have become apparent.

Often the host country (that is, the country where a multi-national corporation is operating) may not have sufficient protections in place safeguarding human rights. Accordingly, when adverse impacts result from a corporation's activities in that country, the legal mechanisms under which victims might seek redress are either inadequate or non-existent.

Even where appropriate laws and regulations are in place, in many cases the public institutions responsible for law enforcement in the host country may be unwilling or unable to enforce them. There are myriad reasons for this, including corruption, nepotism, or institutional weakness or failure. In addition, there may simply be a reticence to impose harsh penalties and judgements on a foreign corporation out of the fear that it – and others like it – will take its lucrative and much-needed investment in the economy elsewhere.

Meanwhile, in the home country (that is, the corporation's country of origin), there is often a reluctance to exercise extraterritorial jurisdiction over the activities of its corporations operating in far-flung corners of the world. Again, there are several reasons for this. They include the practical difficulties of locating evidence and witnesses in a foreign country to prosecute a case against the corporation concerned. As a result, the home country will often defer to the host country's laws and procedures, even where these may be inadequate.

These profound gaps in governance have meant that, in many instances, neither the home nor the host country has provided redress for victims affected by corporate violations of human rights. It is against this backdrop that the business and human rights field took root and eventually blossomed into what it is today.

Most saliently, business and human rights came to global prominence in June 2011 when the United Nations' Human Rights Council unanimously endorsed Harvard Professor John Ruggie's Guiding Principles on Transnational Business and Human Rights (Guiding Principles).[3]

The Guiding Principles are significant as they represent two firsts:

1   they are the first authoritative guidance that the UN Human Rights Council, or its predecessor, the Human Rights Commission, has ever issued on business and human rights; and
2   it was the first time that the Human Rights Council had ever endorsed any normative document, on any subject, that governments had not negotiated themselves.[4]

There are 31 Guiding Principles. They outline how States can meet their duty to protect human rights, and how corporations can meet their responsibility to respect human rights.

The Guiding Principles are underpinned by the "Protect, Respect and Remedy" Framework (the Framework),[5] also developed by Professor Ruggie. The Framework comprises three pillars:

1   the State duty to protect against human rights abuses by third parties – including business enterprises – through appropriate policies, regulation and adjudication;
2   the corporate responsibility to respect human rights, which means that business enterprises should act with due diligence to avoid infringing on the rights of others and to address the adverse impacts with which they are involved; and

3   the need for victims to have greater access to effective remedy, both judicial and non-judicial, including State-based and non-State-based mechanisms.

The Guiding Principles and the Framework are discussed in greater detail throughout this book. Both are central to a proper understanding of the business and human rights area.

While the Guiding Principles' endorsement is seen by many as the high watermark of business and human rights, it is important to underscore that business and human rights issues have existed in one form or another for decades, indeed for as long as business has interacted with, and impacted on, society. Its precursors in the corporate social responsibility field and within the United Nations system will be outlined to place recent developments in context.

Notes

1 *International Covenant on Civil and Political Rights*, Dec. 16, 1966, S. Treaty Doc. No. 95–20, 6 I.L.M. 368 (1967), 999 U.N.T.S. 171.
2 *International Covenant on Economic, Social and Cultural Rights*, Dec. 16, 1966, S. Treaty Doc. No. 95–19, 6 I.L.M. 360 (1967), 993 U.N.T.S. 3.
3 Guiding Principles on Business and Human Rights: Implementing the United Nations' "Protect, Respect and Remedy" Framework, A/HRC/17/31: 21 March 2011.
4 Ruggie, J. "Opening statement at the First Annual UN Forum on Business and Human Rights," Geneva, 3–5 December 2012. Accessed on 9 March 2018: www.ohchr.org/EN/Issues/Business/Forum/Pages/2012ForumonBusinessandHumanRights.aspx.
5 Ruggie, J. "Protect, respect and remedy: a Framework for Business and Human Rights," A/HRC/8/5: 7 April 2008.

Chapter 2

How this book is structured

Human rights are a compelling issue for *all* businesses to consider, irrespective of their size, sector, location, ownership, or structure. Despite this, the human rights risks faced by any one corporation will vary greatly depending on the complexity of its supply chain, the country or countries in which it operates, and the nature of its industry, among many other factors.

To set the scene for the discussion that follows, Part II of this book examines the evolving social and economic context in which business's detrimental impacts on human rights have occurred. This has been impacted by various interconnecting phenomena including (among others) the globalisation of markets; increasingly complex and disparate supply chains; and governance gaps in many emerging nations where multinational corporations are operating.

Part II also clarifies some of the similarities and differences between the area of business and human rights and corporate social responsibility more broadly. It also outlines the concept of creating shared value, which some commentators claim has superseded corporate social responsibility. Having done so, it outlines the development of the Guiding Principles, and their precursors in the United Nations system.

Part III of the book analyses the implications for business of human rights – from both a legal and non-legal perspective. In addition, it considers some of the implications for business of recent developments in the areas of modern slavery and sexual assault and harassment.

Given the fluid and rapidly evolving nature of the business and human rights field, business's obligations (and the expectations on business) are changing with each passing year. This demands that corporations take a proactive and agile approach in managing these issues.

With this background in mind, Part IV addresses what kinds of actions a company should take to actively start addressing the human rights-related risks in its business and supply chain.

Lastly, Part V provides some illustrative case studies or "snapshots" from four very different industries: apparel, fast-moving consumer goods, electronics, and banking. These case studies put the theory into context, depicting some of the real-life human rights challenges businesses face and how they have tried (and sometimes failed) to address them.

Part VI concludes with some suggestions of where to go from here.

Part II

Business and human rights in context

Chapter 3

The social and economic context

Corporations now make up more than two-thirds of the world's top economies.[1] As such, they have enormous potential to impact on human rights whether for better or for worse. Similarly, a human rights disaster can irreparably damage a corporation's reputation and financial bottom-line, having a long-lasting impact on its future.

To better understand this dynamic and how it has changed in recent years, it is useful to highlight some key features of the social and economic context in which corporations operate.

Globalisation

Perhaps more than any other feature, globalisation has played a critical role in transforming modern societies and their economies. In simple terms, globalisation is the increasing interaction of people, States, or countries through an increased flow of money, ideas, and culture. While it is primarily an economic process of integration, it also has social and cultural aspects.

In his bestselling book, *The World Is Flat*, Thomas L. Friedman comments on the transformative nature and levelling effects of globalisation. He states: "[m]ore people can plug, play, compete, connect, and collaborate with more equal power than ever before."[2]

Similarly, he states:

> In my view, this flattening of the playing field is the most
> important thing happening in the world today, and those
> who get caught up in measuring globalization purely by
> trade statistics – or as a purely economic phenomenon
> instead of one that affects everything from individual
> empowerment to culture to how hierarchical institutions
> operate – are missing the impact of this change.[3]

From the perspective of the corporation, globalisation has presented unprecedented opportunities to obtain goods and services
from different locations around the globe, taking advantage of
the best options in terms of cost and quality. An excellent
example of the global value chain in action is provided by Boe-
ing's 787 Dreamliner.

The Dreamliner is assembled from myriad component parts,
sourced from different companies around the world. Suppliers
include companies from Japan, Korea, Australia, USA, UK, Italy,
France, Canada, and Sweden. Indeed, in some cases, parts for the
Dreamliner originate from several locations (and sometimes several
companies) within the one country. For example, parts come from
at least seven different locations within the USA – Auburn, Washington; Frederickson, Washington; Charleston, South Carolina;
Tulsa, Oklahoma; Evendale, Ohio; Wichita, Kansas; and Chula
Vista, California – and from at least five different companies in the
USA. Once, it would not have been feasible (either logistically or
financially) to source aeroplane parts from such an array of countries and companies around the globe. Now, it is not only feasible
but often preferable from a cost and quality perspective.

In terms of "services," the opportunities globalisation has
afforded for corporations to readily tap into cheaper offshore
labour markets have also been a game-changer with significant
implications both socially and economically for workers in home
and host countries. The American industry-led Reshoring Initiative estimates that three to five million manufacturing jobs in
the US have been lost to trade/offshoring since 1979.[4] Of these, it

is estimated that around 1.4 million manufacturing jobs were lost between 2007 and 2014 during the administration of President Obama, which supported free trade.[5] Some estimates indicate that approximately one-third of these jobs have gone to China.[6]

Trump appealed to many of these disgruntled former manufacturing workers in his so-called "trade war" with China. He promised to restore the American dream by "Making America Great Again." A popular view promulgated by the media is that a "Rustbelt revolt" by white working-class voters catapulted Trump into the White House in the 2016 election. This is not quite correct. Instead, it was actually the collapse of Democratic support in former manufacturing hubs – as huge numbers of Democrat voters either stayed home or voted for a third party – that was determinative.[7]

However, the trend towards offshoring has slowed in recent years. As labour costs have risen steadily around the world, corporations have had to counterbalance the benefits of (relatively) lower labour and operating costs in foreign countries with the disadvantages of offshoring – including increased shipping costs and time to transport goods, and diminished flexibility to respond to changes in customer demand.

On the positive side, the benefits of globalisation extend beyond a company's ability to optimise the costs and quality of the goods and services it purchases. In addition, by establishing operations in other countries, such as China, companies have gained access to lucrative new markets without the hurdle of trade barriers. As Friedman observes, nearly 90 per cent of the output from American-owned offshore factories is sold to foreign consumers.[8] In turn (and contrary to public perception), this stimulates American exports and American jobs. Further, for consumers in the companies' home countries there are the clear benefits of lower prices for goods manufactured in China and other developing countries (although this situation is currently evolving with the introduction of President Trump's more protectionist trade policies).

While the ability to source goods and services from a plethora of suppliers around the globe brings clear benefits, there are also potential downsides of supply chains that are dispersed and

labyrinthine. One of the most significant disadvantages of globalisation is the extent to which it has precipitated governance
gaps around business's adverse impacts on human rights. For
example, in many cases the host country may not have sufficient
protections in place safeguarding human rights abuses by individuals or corporate actors. This is problematic both from the
perspective of preventing corporate human rights abuses and for
addressing their impacts after they occur.

Alternatively, even where there *are* laws and regulations in
place in a host country to deal with human rights-related complaints, the public institutions responsible for law enforcement
in the host country may be unwilling or unable to enforce them.
This may be due to corruption, nepotism, or institutional weakness or failure. In some cases, there may simply be a reticence
to impose harsh penalties and judgments on a foreign corporation out of the fear that it – and others like it – will be dis-
suaded from investing in that country and take its business
elsewhere.

If the host country is unable or unwilling to prevent or redress
corporate human rights abuses, victims may turn to the "home"
country of the multinational corporation. However, this too
presents difficulties in many cases. While a home country can
choose to exercise extraterritorial (or international) jurisdiction
over corporations domiciled in its jurisdiction, in general it is
not required to do so. The UN Guiding Principles state as
follows:

> At present States are not generally required under inter-
> national human rights law to regulate the extraterritorial
> activities of businesses domiciled in their territory and/or jur-
> isdiction. Nor are they generally prohibited from doing so,
> provided there is a recognized jurisdictional basis.[9]

Practically, it can be very difficult for the home country to locate
sufficient supporting evidence and witnesses to successfully prosecute one of its corporations for its activities overseas. Further,
considerations of international law – such as the concept of State

sovereignty[10] and *forum non conveniens*[11] – will in many cases militate against the assertion by the home State of jurisdiction over one of its corporations adversely impacting human rights in another country.

Accordingly, in multinational supply chains weaving a complex web of intersecting relationships across the globe, there are many instances where neither the host nor home State will act to either prevent or address the adverse impacts of corporations on human rights.

In recent years, two new developments related to globalisation have also generated significant concern. The first is the manipulation of information – both online and offline – in a way that favours the powerful and elites. This stands in stark contrast to the "equal power" Friedman celebrated in *The World Is Flat* and is reflected in new efforts to curtail internet neutrality as well as Russian and other campaigns to shape the information environment.

In its April 2017 report, *Information Operations and Facebook*, Facebook confirmed that during the 2016 US presidential election it detected and monitored efforts by malicious actors to manipulate US citizens and, in turn, to effect the outcome of the election.[12] According to Facebook's report, these nefarious efforts took a range of forms including:

- Publishing stolen data: private information was accessed and stolen from systems outside of Facebook. Sites hosting this data were then registered and subsequently promoted through the other methods below.
- False (or fake) news: news articles purporting to be factual, but which contained intentional misstatements of fact with the intention to arouse passions, attract viewership, or deceive.
- False amplifiers: coordinated activity by inauthentic accounts with the intent of manipulating political discussion.
- Disinformation: inaccurate or manipulated information or content that was spread intentionally. (Note: disinformation differs from misinformation, which is the *unintentional* spread of inaccurate information without malicious intent.)[13]

In its 2017 report, Facebook stated it "is not in a position to make definitive attribution to the actors sponsoring this activity." However, it also said, "our data does not contradict the attribution provided by the U.S. Director of National Intelligence in the report dated January 6, 2017."[14] The US National Intelligence Report assessed with high confidence that Russian president Vladimir Putin orchestrated the campaign to influence the outcome of the US election. It stated:

> Russia's goals were to undermine public faith in the US democratic process, denigrate Secretary Clinton, and harm her electability and potential presidency. We further assess Putin and the Russian Government developed a clear preference for President-elect Trump.[15]

Another example of how information globalisation has been manipulated by powerful elites to impact geopolitical events is Russia's interference in the 2016 Brexit referendum in the United Kingdom. Russia sought to influence the Brexit campaign through various means, including disinformation, cyber hacking, and corruption.

In July 2018, the House of Commons' Culture, Media and Sport Select Committee released its interim report, *Disinformation and "Fake News."* It found that Russia had engaged in "unconventional warfare" through Twitter and other social media against the United Kingdom, designed to amplify support for a "leave" vote in Brexit.[16] This is consistent with comments made by the British prime minister, Theresa May, at the Lord Mayor's Banquet in November 2017. Prime Minister May accused Russia of meddling in elections and planting fake news in an attempt to "weaponise information" and sow discord in the West.[17]

A second challenging development is the emergence of a new corporatism in which many corporations are arms of State policy (in the Chinese model) or where the State and corporations form a combined oligarchy (in the Russian model). Under both models there is an inherent conflict of interest present when a

State regulates corporations and, at the same time, owns the regulated entity. Understandably, there is concern that States could use their political power to benefit the economic activities of their State-owned enterprises (SOEs).

In China, there are approximately 150,000 SOEs,[18] comprising 80 per cent of the value of the Chinese stock market.[19] Historically, SOEs (or government-owned corporations) were formed after the People's Republic of China was founded in 1949 and the State seized control of all businesses. Given their dual commercial and policy roles, SOEs are notorious for being less efficient than their private-sector counterparts. Additionally, some critics argue that having such a large share of economic activity controlled by SOEs "means larger potential for corruption, lower potential for innovation and a smaller range of opportunities for people to pursue different careers and lifestyles."[20]

Following the 2008 global financial crisis, the Chinese Government initiated a programme of spending to stimulate the economy. Much of the money was invested in SOEs and, more specifically, in infrastructure projects. Despite the positive short-term benefits of the stimulus spending, it was financed by enormous debt that now threatens to undermine China's economic stability. Indeed, at the National Financial Work Conference in July 2017, President Xi Jinping stated that the SOE debt problem is the "priority of priorities."[21]

In Russia, most important economic assets in the country are controlled by former State security and intelligence officials (or secret police).[22] As a result, an oligarchy exists whereby economic and political power is monopolised by a few leading figures. The implications for democracy, human rights, and the rule of law are significant. As a former adviser to Vladimir Putin, Andrei Illarionov, has described:

> The strengthening of the corporativist state model and setting up favorable conditions for quasi-state monopolies by the state itself hurt the economy.... Cabinet members or key Presidential Staff executives chairing corporation boards or serving on those boards are the order of the day in Russia. In

what Western country – except in the corporativist state that lasted for 20 years in Italy – is such a phenomenon possible? Which, actually, proves that the term "corporativist" properly applies to Russia today. We are witnessing aggression on the part of quasi-state run corporations against whatever private businesses capable of generating cash flows.[23]

From a business and human rights perspective, significant complexities can arise when corporations are government-owned and/or -controlled. Given the different obligations on States and businesses under the UN Guiding Principles to (respectively) protect and respect human rights, confusion around the scope and intersection of these obligations can occur when a corporation is fully or partly government-owned. A pertinent example of this is given by Professor Larry Catá Backer of Pennsylvania State University in his 2017 article on the human rights obligations of SOEs. He describes the challenging scenario where a SOE has breached an obligation under the *International Covenant on Civil and Political Rights* ("ICCPR"), yet its State has not implemented that treaty under its domestic law. He states:

> Because of the nature of the relationship between SOE and state, that breach can be attributed to the state. But the state in question has not incorporated the ICCPR in its domestic legal order. Under these circumstances the SOE has breached its responsibility, but has the state breached its duty? This can be seen as a back door way of imposing international law on states otherwise unwilling to consent to its adoption. But states will tend to reject this as inconsistent with international law.[24]

While not addressing this specific scenario, UN Guiding Principle 4 provides general guidance to States on how to manage the State–business nexus where SOEs are concerned. It provides:

> States should *take additional steps to protect against human rights abuses by business* enterprises that are *owned or*

controlled by the State, or that receive substantial support
and services from State agencies such as export credit agencies and official investment insurance or guarantee agencies,
including, where appropriate, by requiring human rights due
diligence [emphases added].[25]

As the Commentary to UN Guiding Principle 4 explains, an
abuse of human rights by a State-owned (or -controlled) business
enterprise may entail a violation of the State's own international
law obligations. Further, the closer a business enterprise is to the
State, the stronger the State's policy rationale is for ensuring that
it respects human rights.

Other problems and challenges to consider, in the context of
SOEs, include the corporate personality of the business enterprise
and whether it (through the State) has any claim to sovereign
immunity. While a SOE is (in theory) autonomous and independent, it is at the same time an instrument of the State. When
the two concepts are conflated, there is the real possibility that
an SOE can seek to evade its responsibility to respect human
rights by relying on the State's sovereign immunity, invariably
resulting in a setback for the protection of human rights.

The two developments outlined above – information globalisation and the proliferation of State-owned or -controlled enterprises – were not properly understood in the past. Now,
awareness of these factors shapes and transforms our view of the
multinational corporation and its role in globalisation.

Political uncertainty and instability

It is ironic that another key feature characterising the current
environment in which corporations operate – political uncertainty and instability – stands as a counterbalance to globalisation and could, in fact, lead to de-globalisation as trade and
investment between countries diminish.

In the decade or so following the global financial crisis, dis-
affection has fermented among various groups in society who are
unhappy with the status quo. While inequality has been falling

consistently in industrialised nations since the beginning of the twentieth century, since the 1980s the share of income going to the top 1 per cent has increased in the United States, United Kingdom, Canada, Ireland, and Australia.[26]

Outside the top 1 per cent, many people have experienced great losses – financially, professionally, and personally – due to the financial crisis and yearn for radical change. This discontent has precipitated the Occupy Movement, an international socio-political movement against social and economic inequality around the world. The movement has adopted the slogan "We are the 99%" and seeks to effect change by highlighting corporate greed. It is premised on the belief that large corporations disproportionately benefit a small minority at the expense of the majority, and of democracy.

At the same time, we have seen a surge of far-right political parties (and leaders) in various parts of the world. German researchers Manuel Funke, Moritz Schularick, and Christoph Trebesch argue that far-right parties are the biggest beneficiaries of financial crises. Their research uses a dataset that covers elections and crises in 20 advanced economies going back to 1870 to systematically study the political aftermath of financial crises. Their study demonstrates that the typical outcome of financial crises is: "votes for far-right parties increase strongly, government majorities shrink, the fractionalisation of parliaments rises and the overall number of parties represented in parliament jumps."[27]

Around the world, significant uncertainty and instability have been generated by these concurrent sociopolitical factors. For corporations vilified by the Occupy Movement, there has been a renewed impetus to combat the widespread antipathy against them by demonstrating their corporate citizenship and social responsibility, irrespective of the validity (or otherwise) of the generalised claims made against them by the movement. Meanwhile, corporations in many nations around the world are operating in destabilised political environments, where policy settings have shifted since the financial crisis and parliaments are increasingly fractured. From the perspectives of corporate executives and their boards, this presents clear challenges for predictability as it is uncertain how the laws and regulations applying to them will shift in the future.

Social media and the 24-hour news cycle

Third, social media and the 24-hour news cycle have also been instrumental in reconfiguring the context in which corporations now operate. Corporations' daily activities have come under acute and unrelenting public scrutiny through a plethora of social media channels including Twitter, Facebook, LinkedIn, and YouTube, to name a few. This has augmented the scrutiny they already faced through more traditional media channels: print, online, and broadcast.

When it comes to sensitive matters, such as a corporation's potential impact on human rights, this heightened level of exposure can be dynamite to a corporation's reputation. On the positive side, social media potentially brings greater transparency and accountability to corporations' actions and can also provide a forum to showcase their activities and contributions in this area.

On the negative side, social media's open and largely unregulated nature means that there are fewer filters or checks for the quality and accuracy of the information presented. Further, the fact that the media is ubiquitous and now operates on a 24-hour news cycle means that there can be no respite for corporations seeking to monitor the claims made in the public domain against them. Where once news outlets operated on more predictable time frames – for example, the morning and evening news bulletins; the early and late editions of the newspaper – today these parameters have been upended such that corporations need to exercise constant vigilance in monitoring the news presented about them across a variety of media platforms.

Like globalisation and an unstable political environment, these developments in social media and the 24-hour news cycle have completely transformed the context in which corporations now operate. Where once a corporation's reputation and public image could be more closely planned and stage managed, today the risks of exposure to public scrutiny and disapprobation – whether justified or not – are far greater.

Notes

1 The World Bank, "The world's top 100 economies: 31 countries; 69 corporations," 20 September 2016. Accessed on 14 July 2018: https://blogs.worldbank.org/publicsphere/world-s-top-100-economies-31-countries-69-corporations.

2 Thomas L. Friedman, *The World Is Flat*, Penguin Books, 2007, p. 6.

3 As above.

4 Reshoring Initiative, "How many jobs have been lost to offshoring, and can be recovered by reshoring?" 10 March 2017. Accessed on 19 July 2018: http://reshorenow.org/blog/how-many-jobs-have-been-lost-to-offshoring-and-can-be-recovered-by-reshoring.

5 Faber, Daniel, Stephens, Jennie, Wallis, Victor, Gottlieb, Roger, Levenstein, Charles, CoatarPeter, Patrick, & Boston Editorial Group of CNS. "Trump's electoral triumph: Class, race, gender, and the hegemony of the polluter-industrial complex." *Capitalism Nature Socialism*, vol. 28, no. 1, 2017, pp. 1–15, DOI: 10.1080/10455752. 2017.1279867. Accessed on 9 September 2018: https://doi.org/10.10 80/10455752.2017.1279867, p. 5.

6 Kellogg Insight, "How much does it cost to manufacture overseas versus at home?" 10 July 2017. Accessed on 19 July 2018: https://insight.kellogg.northwestern.edu/article/how-much-does-it-cost-to-manufacture-overseas-versus-at-home.

7 Faber, Daniel, Stephens, Jennie, Wallis, Victor, Gottlieb, Roger, Levenstein, Charles, CoatarPeter, Patrick, & Boston Editorial Group of CNS. "Trump's electoral triumph: Class, race, gender, and the hegemony of the polluter-industrial complex." *Capitalism Nature Socialism*, vol. 28, no. 1, 2017, pp. 1–15, DOI: 10.1080/10455752.2017. 1279867. Accessed on 9 September 2018: https://doi.org/10.1080/10 455752.2017.1279867, p. 4.

8 Friedman, as above, note 7, p. 135.

9 UN Guiding Principle 2.

10 State sovereignty is the concept that States are in complete and exclusive control of all the people and property within their territory. State sovereignty also includes the idea that all States are equal as States.

11 *Forum non conveniens* is a discretionary power that allows courts to dismiss a case where another court, or forum, is much better suited to hear the case.

12 Weedon, J., Nuland, W., and Stamos, A., *Information Operations and Facebook*, 27 April 2017, version 1.0, p. 11.
13 As above, pp. 5 and 11.
14 As above, p. 11.
15 Office of the Director of National Intelligence, *Background to "Assessing Russian Activities and Intentions in Recent US Elections": The Analytic Process and Cyber Incident Attribution*, 6 January 2017, p. ii. Accessed on 28 August 2018: www.dni.gov/files/documents/ICA_2017_01.pdf.
16 House of Commons, Culture, Media and Sport Select Committee, *Disinformation and "Fake News": Interim Report* (July 2018), Chapter 5.
17 Mason, Rowena. "Theresa May accuses Russia of interfering in elections and fake news," *Guardian*, 14 November 2017. Accessed on 1 September 2018: www.theguardian.com/politics/2017/nov/13/theresa-may-accuses-russia-of-interfering-in-elections-and-fake-news.
18 Nunlist, Tom. "Piece by piece: SOE reform is among China's biggest challenges," *CKGSB Knowledge*, 1 November 2017. Accessed on 1 September 2018: http://knowledge.ckgsb.edu.cn/2017/11/01/chinese-economy/state-owned-enterprise-reform-china.
19 Catá Backer, Larry. "The human rights obligations of state-owned enterprises: Emerging conceptual structures and principles in national and international law and policy." *Vanderbilt Journal of Transnational Law*, vol. 50 no. 4, October 2017, p. 850. Accessed on 8 September 2018: www.vanderbilt.edu/jotl/wp-content/uploads/sites/78/5.-Backer_Final-Review.pdf.
20 Andrew Batson, Gavekal Dragonomics cited by Tom Nunlist. As above.
21 As above.
22 Anderson, Julie. "The Chekist takeover of the Russian state." *International Journal of Intelligence and Counter-Intelligence*, vol. 19, no. 2, 2006, pp. 237–288.
23 Zarakhovich, Yuri. "Q&A: Putin's critical adviser." *Time Magazine*, 31 December 2005.
24 As above, Larry Catá Backer, p. 863.
25 UN Guiding Principles, Principle 4, p. 6.
26 Roser, Max (2018) – "Global economic inequality." *Published online at OurWorldInData.org*. Accessed on 20 July 2018: https://ourworldindata.org/global-economic-inequality.
27 Funke, M., Schularick, M., and Trebesch, C. "Going to extremes: Politics after financial crises, 1870–2014," CEPR, Discussion Paper No. 10884, 2015.

Chapter 4

Corporate social responsibility versus business and human rights

Debates about the social responsibility of corporations have been around for decades. During this time, various terms have emerged to refer to business's impacts on society and ways to address them. In addition to corporate social responsibility ("CSR"), they include: corporate citizenship, corporate sustainability, social innovation, conscious capitalism, and creating shared value. In many respects, these areas have progressed a long way. In other ways, they have not evolved as far as one might have hoped.

This chapter provides a broad overview of some of the key concepts and debates. It clarifies their interaction with (and divergence from) the field of business and human rights. In particular, it discusses the concept of creating shared value ("CSV"), which has been enthusiastically embraced by many multinationals and, many would argue, has now superseded CSR. My analysis focuses on CSV in preference to the other concepts mentioned above as, along with business and human rights, CSV has emerged as a preeminent framework adopted by companies seeking to understand their interactions with, and impacts on, the communities in which they operate.

This chapter closes with a brief discussion of the age-old question "what is the business case for a corporation to address its adverse impacts on society?" While there are compelling reasons why respecting human rights is indeed good for business, a persistent counter-question remains as the metaphorical elephant in the room ... what if it wasn't?

A range of perspectives

In his seminal article, published in the *New York Times Magazine* in 1970, American economist and Nobel laureate Milton Friedman decried the idea of business having social responsibilities and argued that corporate social responsibility is "pure and unadulterated socialism."[1]

Instead, in a free society, Friedman believed that:

> there is one and only one social responsibility to business – to use its resources and engage in activities designed to increase its profits as long as it stays within the rules of the game, which is to say, engages in open and free competition without deception or fraud.[2]

To Friedman, a free market economy is a collection of individuals who voluntarily participate in society based on their own self-interest and desires. He considered that individual agency is subverted by the doctrine of social responsibility which professes "to believe that collectivist ends can be attained without collectivist means."[3]

In other words, by assuming social responsibilities, corporate executives are playing the role of an unelected government: spending other people's money (in most cases, shareholders' and the business owners') for social purposes.

A different perspective is provided by Kenneth Goodpaster and John Matthews. In their article, published in the *Harvard Business Review* in 1982, they argue that it is not sufficient to draw a sharp line between individuals' private ideas and efforts and a corporation's institutional efforts.[4] Instead, the latter should be built on the former. Rationality and respect are the components of individual responsibility.

They believe that these concepts can and should be applied to a corporation equally, and that corporations should be no more and no less morally responsible than individuals. In essence, Goodpaster and Matthews's frame of reference for thinking about and implementing corporate social responsibility is to spell out the processes associated with the moral responsibility of individuals and then to project them directly onto organisations.

More recently, Professor Aneel Karnani, in his article "The Case Against Corporate Social Responsibility," discussed the alignment of profits and social welfare. In his view, social responsibility is usually determined by what is most expedient for a corporation. He states:

> Very simply, in cases where private profits and public interests are aligned, the idea of corporate social responsibility is irrelevant: Companies that simply do everything they can to boost profits will end up increasing social welfare. In circumstances in which profits and social welfare are in direct opposition, an appeal to corporate social responsibility will almost always be ineffective, because executives are unlikely to act voluntarily in the public interest and against shareholder interests.[5]

Based on this view, doing what is best for society usually means sacrificing profits. If this was not the case, he argues, then logically most of society's problems would have already been solved long ago.

Notably, both Karnani and Friedman make a distinction for privately owned companies. If an owner-operated business chooses to accept diminished profits, that is not a decision that has been imposed on its shareholders, and so is unproblematic.

Interestingly – and contrary to Karnani's argument – the idea of maximising economic value for a company in a way that creates value for society by addressing its needs and challenges has been resurrected in recent years through the concept of creating shared value ("CSV").

CSV was popularised by Harvard Business School professor Michael E. Porter and Mark R. Kramer in their *Harvard Business Review* articles.[6] As a side note, Professor Porter, as the most cited scholar today in economics and business, is a formidable authority with extraordinary influence in both business and academia.

Making the ambitious claim that "CSV resets the boundaries of capitalism," Porter and Kramer define CSV as:

> The policies and operating practices that enhance the competitiveness of a company while simultaneously advancing the economic and social conditions in the communities in which it operates.[7]

CSV aims to supersede CSR: enabling companies to generate increased profits by creating societal value. In Porter and Kramer's model, companies can do this in several ways:

1   *By reconceiving their products and markets*: this is achieved by seizing opportunities to better meet the needs of their underserved customers, particularly in developing economies, including Brazil, India, and China. While these markets were once generally overlooked as unviable, CSV argues that corporations can tap into new, billion-dollar markets, thereby increasing their profits while also providing a social benefit to these communities.

    To do this, a company may need to redesign its products and/or services, or to rethink its distribution methods. One example the authors give is microfinance, which was invented to meet the need many people in developing countries had for a source of business finance.

2   *By redefining productivity in the value chain*: social problems can incur costs to a company in its own value chain. For example, excess packaging and greenhouse gas emissions not only impact the environment detrimentally but also impose costs on a business. Porter and Kramer cite the case of Walmart, which, in 2009, addressed both issues by reducing its packaging and rerouting its trucks to cut 100 million miles from its delivery routes. In doing so, it saved $200 million, despite shipping more products that year.[8]

3   *By enabling local cluster development*: companies' productivity and innovation are improved by having supportive

companies and infrastructure around them. In addition to other businesses, Porter and Kramer argue that this includes institutions and public assets, such as schools, universities, clean water, fair competition laws, quality standards, and market transparency.[9]

How useful is CSV?

Porter and Kramer's achievement is significant. By recasting the discussion in terms of the opportunities for business to innovate to meet society's needs, while at the same time generating business profits, they have catalysed a global corporate movement motivated by these twin goals.

Indeed, the concept of CSV has been enthusiastically received and adopted by many multinational corporations, including GE, Nestlé, Coca-Cola, Walmart, Novo Nordisk, and Inditex. The Shared Value Initiative ("SVI") was established in 2012 and serves as a global knowledge and learning hub for companies and other stakeholders interested in developing CSV strategies. Each year SVI hosts the Shared Value Leadership Summit, a three-day conference bringing together eminent leaders from business, government, academia, and the not-for-profit sector. In addition to Porter and Kramer, speakers at the 2018 summit included Hillary Rodham Clinton, and CEOs and senior executives from a host of Fortune 500 companies.

But despite its apparent success, CSV has been critiqued from various perspectives. A 2011 article in *The Economist* argued that it was "undercooked" and lacking in empirical evidence.[10] Specifically, the author assailed the concept of CSV (and Porter, in particular) on the basis that it/he (and presumably Kramer also) add nothing new to corporations' understanding of their social and economic impacts, and the risks of "short-termist" thinking. The article states:

> There is a striking similarity between shared value and Jed Emerson's concept of blended value, in which firms seek simultaneously to pursue profit and social and environmental

targets. There is also an overlap with Stuart Hart's 2005 book, "Capitalism at the Crossroads."[11]

Similarly, Professors Andrew Crane and Dirk Matten (along with their co-authors Guido Palazzo and Laura J. Spence) have strongly criticised CSV on the basis that it is unoriginal and fails to acknowledge the literature on which it draws. In addition, they argue that it ignores the inherent tensions between social and economic goals, is naïve about business compliance, and is based on a shallow conception of the corporation's role in society.[12]

In a back-and-forth response and counter-response to Crane *et al.*, published in *California Management Review*, Porter and Kramer counter their criticisms by stating:

> We think the reason our article has drawn so much attention is that it provides an overall, strategic view of how to think about the role of the corporation in society, which not only incorporates and extends past scholarship on corporate philanthropy, CSR, and sustainability, but also distinguishes CSV as a distinct, powerful, and transformational model that is embedded in the core purpose of the corporation.[13]

While acknowledging related streams of work, Porter and Kramer contend that "related work does not mean that the concepts are the same."[14] Further, they consider that Crane *et al.* misunderstand their arguments regarding CSV's presumption of compliance with legal and ethical standards. While Porter and Kramer write in their articles that legal compliance is a prerequisite, they argue that "the concept of shared value takes company behavior much further."[15]

Crane *et al.* have the final say in the *California Management Review* exchange. They pointedly comment on Porter and Kramer's response that: "there is little in their response to assuage any skepticism one might have about the value of their framework."[16] In relation to Porter and Kramer's contention that obeying the law and behaving ethically are prerequisites to CSV, they state:

"The so-called 'prerequisites' are where Porter and Kramer are hiding all the tough challenges. It is a classic economist's trick of assuming away all the messy stuff that is difficult to deal with."[17]

There is certainly no love lost between the camps of Crane *et al.*, and Porter and Kramer. On various issues, both sides appear to feel that their position has been misunderstood or wilfully misrepresented by the other. It all seems to end at an impasse. Ultimately, there appear to be valid perspectives expressed on both sides; the truth perhaps lies somewhere in between.

Perhaps more so than any other corporate social responsibility model or framework in recent times, CSV resonates very strongly with many corporations around the world. It has engendered greater understanding of corporations' social and economic impacts in boardrooms and offices globally and has spurred on corporate projects that have undoubtedly led to positive outcomes both financially and socially.

However, this does not invalidate the arguments made by CSV's detractors, as articulated by Andrew Crane and his co-authors. Porter and Kramer's *HBR* articles present CSV as a slick, marketable concept that is appealing and quickly digestible by the busy corporate executive. But, in doing so, they tend to gloss over many of the complexities and intrinsic tensions between social and economic goals.

Clearly, there will be many instances where it will *not* be profitable for a company to meet society's needs, even where these needs are compelling. In many cases, particularly in the short-term, it will be costly and time-consuming to do so. Likewise, in assuming legal compliance as a given, CSV makes a huge assumption. In a perfect world, this would be less problematic. However, given the frequency of corporate malfeasance and unlawful action across various industries, it seems unrealistic and a leap too far.

Keeping these benefits and limitations on both sides of the ledger in mind, we now turn to consider the relevance of CSV to the business and human rights area.

How does CSV relate to business and human rights?

Given the natural corollaries and apparent overlap between CSV and the UN Guiding Principles, and the fact that both emerged at around the same time,[18] you might expect some cross-pollination between the two areas. Curiously, though, human rights have not been a significant feature in discussions of CSV (or, before that, CSR more broadly). Similarly, the concept of CSV seems to have been largely overlooked by the Guiding Principles and the Commentary on them.

There are three main reasons for this:

1   *A difference in focus*: while the Guiding Principles concentrate on business *risk*, CSV is driven by business *opportunity*.
2   *A difference in rationale*: while both are *voluntary* and do not create any additional legal obligations on business directly, the Guiding Principles operate to enhance due diligence processes and minimise legal exposure, whereas CSV takes legal compliance for granted.
3   *The optics of human rights*: there is a perception among many people that human rights have negative connotations and are incompatible with business opportunity.

Each of these reasons is extrapolated in more detail below.

I Business risk versus opportunity

First, there is an underlying difference in focus. While the Guiding Principles concentrate on business risk, CSV is driven by business opportunity.

In his book *Just Business: Multinational Corporations and Human Rights*, John Ruggie discusses the evolution of corporate philanthropy and social responsibility over time. He confirms the divide that has emerged between business risk and opportunity:

> [t]wo distinct strands emerge, focused on business opportunity and risk respectively. With regard to the first, social

entrepreneurs began to experiment with microenterprises such as consumer lending and mobile telephones or other forms of what came to be known as "bottom of the pyramid marketing" or "social inclusive business models." Most recently, Harvard business guru Michael Porter has advocated a grand strategy of "creating shared value" – companies creating economic value for themselves "in a way that also creates value for society by addressing its needs and challenges." My mandate was meant to encompass the second and less glamorous CSR strand: the risk that companies cause or contribute to adverse social impacts.[19]

In practice, this means that the same situation could be interpreted quite differently depending on whether a shared value or human rights lens is applied.

From a shared value perspective, considerations of opportunity relative to cost are central for a company. For example, gender or race discrimination reduces the pool of capable employees; poverty limits demand for products and can lead to unhealthy workers and increased medical and security costs; poor public education imposes productivity and greater training costs.

However, from the perspective of the Guiding Principles, each of these is first and foremost a human rights issue. They expose a company to legal and reputational risks (if they are in some way involved in causing or contributing to them), independent of the consequential financial costs they are also likely to incur for the business.

I do not contend that Porter and Kramer's model negates human rights; rather it assumes corporate respect for human rights, and for any applicable law, as a given. Indeed, they state: "Creating shared value presumes compliance with the law and ethical standards, as well as mitigating any harm caused by the business, but goes far beyond that."[20] This is one reason for its limited intersection with the field of business and human rights.

2 Role of voluntarism

Another reason for the lack of interaction between the Guiding Principles and CSV can be traced to the difference in their fundamental rationales.

Both are voluntary; the Guiding Principles as a voluntary multi-stakeholder initiative and CSV as a corporate strategy. However, closer examination reveals the situation is more complex. These complexities are interwoven with the nature of human rights as legal obligations, under international law and in many domestic legal systems.

Professor Florian Wettstein has analysed the disjuncture between corporate social responsibility and human rights in terms of voluntariness: the former being seen as optional, discretionary and philanthropic, while human rights are inherently legal obligations.

He argues, "I believe this perception of CSR as something 'fundamentally' voluntary is directly tied to the relative lack of attention it has given to human rights."[21] That is, because many corporations understand CSR as something voluntary and beyond the law, it necessarily excludes human rights from its scope.

Similarly, in analysing the distinctions between CSR, and business and human rights, Professor Anita Ramasastry has written: "CSR focuses on individual company decision making—what human rights scholars and activists might view as an a la carte view of human rights."[22]

In contrast, she states that, under the UN Guiding Principles, "[H]uman Rights due diligence provides companies with a process by which to assess corporate conduct against a universal set of rights. This takes us out of a more a la carte framework or piecemeal approach."[23]

Given that CSV follows in the traditions of CSR, this history is still very relevant to the dynamic between CSV and business and human rights.

Notably, the Universal Declaration of Human Rights explicitly recognises that "human rights should be protected by the rule of law."[24] This has been achieved and developed through human rights treaties and declarations, and their related jurisprudence.

As I discuss in more detail in Chapter 5, the Guiding Principles followed in the wake of the rejected UN Draft Norms on the Responsibilities of Transnational Corporations and other Business Enterprises with Regard to Human Rights ("Draft Norms") and so deliberately opted for a non-binding approach to corporate responsibility for human rights violations.

Nonetheless, the UN Framework and Guiding Principles *do* articulate a global standard that applies to all States and to all companies, and reaffirms the principles of universality, inalienability, interdependence, and indivisibility of human rights. In this sense, it reasserts all the existing legal obligations flowing from the international human rights law regime. In doing so, it seems to broaden the gulf between CSV and the corporate responsibility to respect human rights under the Guiding Principles.

As Wettstein and Ramasastry have argued, there is still room for a larger connection and conversation. It is essential that companies meet their responsibility to respect human rights as articulated by the Guiding Principles; essentially, that they do no harm. But, beyond this, CSV (and CSR) initiatives and State regulations that actually foster or reward the positive fulfilment of human rights by corporations should be increased.

3 Negative connotations of human rights

A third reason for the lack of interaction between CSV and the Guiding Principles appears to be the alienation sometimes created by the concept of "human rights" itself.

This is the case particularly in developed country contexts where there is a widespread assumption that human rights are already fully achieved and are no longer a relevant concern needing to be addressed, or even monitored. In this context, mention of human rights has the potential to lead to defensive or perplexed responses from corporate executives, questioning its relevance.

As a senior executive with a multinational mining company, interviewed as part of my research, commented, "For many people [in companies], 'human rights' is quite alienating. It's considered developing country work and kind of insulting as it brings up connotations of abusive practices, and a lack of development."[25] In extrapolating on the sense of confusion many in the corporate sector feel, this executive commented, "People have a hard time getting their heads around what they're meant to be doing in human rights."[26]

What is the business case for respecting human rights?

Finally, we return to the conspicuous elephant in the room mentioned at the start of this chapter. What is the business case for a corporation to address its adverse impacts on society, and on human rights more specifically?

It is a question many corporate executives would like an answer to. However, from a human rights perspective, it is really the wrong question to be asking. Underlying the question is the presumption that compliance with human rights responsibilities will only be justified if commercial benefits result to a corporation. This is inconsistent with the universality of international human rights standards. It is also inconsistent with the Guiding Principles, under which companies bear a responsibility to respect human rights even in the absence of a clear business case. While the responsibility to respect human rights is distinct from issues of legal liability, it nevertheless applies to *all* corporations, irrespective of their size, sector, location, or presumably the strength of their business case for doing so.

Having said this, there are various compelling reasons why respecting human rights *is* good for business. In a January 2008 special report on corporate responsibility, *The Economist* surmised that paying attention to its social impacts "can amount to enlightened self-interest" for a corporation, and something that over time will help to sustain profits for shareholders.[27] In addition to its shareholders, human rights are increasingly important to numerous other stakeholders in a corporation including its employees, customers, investors, local communities, governments, and civil society groups. A range of positive flow-on effects for each of these groups result from a corporation's decision to respect human rights.

By adopting a proactive approach to managing its adverse impacts on human rights, a company will attract and retain the best and brightest employees who are similarly committed to a progressive vision of the company's role in society. In turn, these employees, believing in their work and their company will be much more engaged and loyal to the organisation over the long term than individuals working for a company that does not emulate their values or imbue their everyday work lives with a larger sense of purpose. Likewise, a company's reputation and brand will be enhanced by its stance on human rights, distinguishing it from its competitors (or at least placing it among the leaders of the pack) and giving it a commercial edge with customers. In terms of investors, the company will be more likely to attract ethical investors who prioritise the importance of environmental, social, and governance ("ESG") risks. Such investors are more likely to be committed to a longer-term perspective on their investment, in turn resulting in a more stable shareholding. In addition, a corporation which genuinely respects human rights is likely to become a valued part of the local communities in which it operates, securing its licence to operate and increasing its acceptance among community members and civil society groups.

In terms of the negative business case, a company that proactively respects human rights will be more likely to avoid costly litigation, shareholder divestment actions and the (sometimes enormous) operational costs of rectifying its detrimental impacts on stakeholders.

Despite the many advantages outlined above, it remains challenging to quantify in financial terms the benefits to a company of respecting human rights. However, one very useful example where this has been achieved successfully is the Shift Project's 2014 report, *Costs of Company-Community Conflict in the Extractives Sector*.[28] The report clearly illustrates the potential costs to extractive companies of failing to prevent or mitigate conflict with local communities connected with their operations. The study analysed publicly available information on 50 situations of prolonged or significant company–community conflict, and 45 in-depth confidential interviews with individuals experienced in the extractives industry.

Some of the study's results were nothing short of astounding. For example, in examining the costs arising from lost productivity due to temporary shutdowns or delay, the report found that:

> a major, world-class mining project with capital expenditure of between US$3–5 billion will suffer costs of roughly US$20 million per week of delayed production in Net Present Value (NPV) terms, largely due to lost sales.[29]

The report found that the greatest costs of conflict were the opportunity costs, such as the lost value linked to future projects, expansion plans, or sales that did not go ahead. The research also found that, even at the early stages of exploration, losses can be sustained, for example from the standing down of drilling programmes.[30]

Similarly, in another case, after a systematic review of non-technical risks connected to its projects (including company–community conflict), a company identified a cost of more than US$6 billion over a two-year period. This cost represented a double-digit percentage of the company's annual profits.[31]

As outlined above, the Guiding Principles have rendered the articulation of a business case for respecting human rights a largely redundant exercise. Nevertheless, doing so undoubtedly affirms the significant qualitative and quantitative returns for a company.

Notes

1 Friedman, Milton. "The social responsibility of business is to increase its profits." *New York Times Magazine*, 11 September 1970, p. 17.
2 Friedman, as above.
3 Friedman, as above.

4 Goodpaster, Kenneth E. and Mathews, John B., Jr., "Can a corporation have a conscience?" *Harvard Business Review on Corporate Responsibility*, 1982, pp. 131–155.

5 Karnani, Aneel. "The case against corporate social responsibility." *Wall Street Journal Europe*, 23 August 2010.

6 Porter, Michael E. and Kramer, Mark R. "Strategy and society: The link between competitive advantage and corporate social responsibility." *HBR*, December 2006; and Porter, Michael E. and Kramer, Mark R. "Creating shared value: How to reinvent capitalism – and unleash a wave of innovation and growth." *HBR*, January–February 2011.

7 Porter and Kramer, as above.

8 Porter and Kramer, as above, p. 9.

9 Porter and Kramer, as above, p. 12.

10 "Oh, Mr Porter." *The Economist*, 10 March 2011. Accessed on 12 June 2018: www.economist.com/node/18330445.

11 *The Economist*, as above.

12 Crane, Andrew, Palazzo, Guido, Spence, Laura J. and Matten, Dirk. "Contesting the value of 'creating shared value.'" *California Management Review*, vol. 56, no. 2, Winter 2014, pp. 130–153.

13 Crane *et al.*, as above, p. 49.

14 Crane *et al.*, as above, p. 49.

15 Crane *et al.*, as above, p. 50.

16 Crane *et al.*, as above, p. 51.

17 Crane *et al.*, as above, p. 52.

18 Professor Ruggie's mandate as UN Special Representative on human rights and transnational corporations and other business enterprises ran from 2005 to 2011. Meanwhile, the concept of creating shared value was popularised by two articles in the *Harvard Business Review* by Porter and Kramer in 2006 and 2011, respectively: "Strategy and society: The link between competitive advantage and corporate social responsibility." *HBR*, December 2006; and "Creating shared value: How to reinvent capitalism – and unleash a wave of innovation and growth." *HBR*, January–February 2011.

19 Ruggie, John Gerard. *Just Business: Multinational Corporations and Human Rights*, W. W. Norton, 2013, p. 69.

20 Porter and Kramer, "Creating shared value: How to reinvent capitalism – and unleash a wave of innovation and growth." *HBR*, January–February 2011.

21 Wettstein, Florian. "CSR and the debate on business and human rights: Bridging the great divide." *Business Ethics Quarterly*, vol. 22, no. 4, October 2012, p. 751.

22 Ramasastry, Anita. "Corporate social responsibility versus business and human rights: Bridging the gap between responsibility and

accountability." *Journal of Human Rights*, vol. 14, no. 237–259, 2015, p. 239.
23 Ramasastry, as above, p. 247.
24 *Universal Declaration of Human Rights*, (UDHR), G.A. Res. 217A(III), U.N. GAOR, 3d Sess., U.N. Doc. A/810 (Dec. 10, 1948).
25 Interview with mining executive (anonymous), 11 March 2014.
26 As above.
27 *The Economist*, "Special report: Do it right: corporate responsibility is largely a matter of enlightened self-interest," 17 January 2008. Accessed on 21 July 2018: www.economist.com/special-report/2008/01/17/do-it-right.
28 Davis, Rachel and Franks, Daniel; Shift and Corporate Responsibility Initiative, Harvard Kennedy School, *Costs of Company-Community Conflict in the Extractives Sector*, May 2014. Accessed on 22 July: www.shiftproject.org/resources/publications/costs-company-community-conflict-extractive-sector.
29 Davis and Franks, as above, p. 8.
30 Davis and Franks, as above.
31 Davis and Franks, as above, p. 24.

Background to the UN Guiding Principles on Business and Human Rights

The previous chapters in Part II have sought to set the scene, both in terms of the economic and social context and in terms of broader developments and thinking on corporate social responsibility (and its successor, shared value). Having done this, Chapter 5 outlines the development of the Guiding Principles, and their precursors in the United Nations system.

Before the Guiding Principles

Since the 1970s, various unsuccessful attempts were made by the UN to clarify corporations' roles and responsibilities in relation to human rights.

In 1973, the UN Commission on Transnational Corporations was set up to establish an international code of conduct for corporations. Unfortunately, this effort failed, as did a subsequent attempt made in the early 1980s.[1]

In 2003, a subcommission of the UN Commission on Human Rights (as the UN Human Rights Council was then known) completed the Draft Norms on the Responsibilities of Transnational Corporations and other Business Enterprises with Regard to Human Rights ("Draft UN Norms").[2]

One of the distinguishing features of the Draft UN Norms was that they attempted to impose *binding* human rights obligations directly on corporate actors. David Weissbrodt, one of the authors of the Draft UN Norms, argued at the time that:

"[T]he legal authority of the Norms derives principally from their sources in treaties and customary international law, as a restatement of international legal principles applicable to companies."[3]

Specifically, the Draft UN Norms stated that business has "the obligation to promote, secure the fulfilment of, respect, ensure respect of, and protect human rights."[4] If the Draft UN Norms had been accepted, this would have meant that corporations had obligations for human rights equivalent to those of governments.

Many non-governmental organisations enthusiastically welcomed the Draft UN Norms as a potentially powerful mechanism to hold corporations accountable for their human rights violations. However, other stakeholders – particularly those in the private sector – were strongly opposed to them. For example, the International Organisation of Employers and the International Chamber of Commerce stated that the Draft UN Norms would "undermine human rights, the business sector of society and the right to development" by inappropriately shifting State responsibilities for human rights to business.[5]

Given the polarised nature of the debate around the Draft UN Norms, it is perhaps unsurprising that the UN Commission on Human Rights abandoned them in 2004. In its decision (which was taken without a vote), the Commission stated that the Draft UN Norms had "no legal standing, and that the Sub-Commission should not perform any monitoring function in this regard."[6]

After this, the lack of clarity surrounding business and human rights remained unresolved. Exactly one year later, on 20 April 2005, the Commission on Human Rights passed a resolution recommending that then UN Secretary-General Kofi Annan appoint an independent expert to "identify and clarify" corporate responsibility for human rights.[7]

A step-change on business and human rights

In 2005, the secretary-general's appointment of Harvard Professor John Ruggie as his special representative on the issue of human rights and transnational corporations and other business enterprises marked a step-change in the UN's efforts to achieve clarity on corporations' responsibilities for human rights.

Professor Ruggie's initial two-year mandate was principally to "identify and clarify standards of corporate responsibility and accountability with regard to human rights,"[8] to elaborate on the role of States in regulating and adjudicating business activities, and to identify examples of best practice.

In his first report to the Human Rights Council in 2007, Ruggie mapped evolving standards, practices, gaps, and trends.[9] In contrast to the Draft UN Norms (which asserted that companies have the same obligations under international human rights law as States), he concluded that:

> [I]t does not seem that the international human rights instruments discussed here currently impose direct legal responsibilities on corporations. Even so, corporations are under growing scrutiny by the international human rights mechanisms.[10]

Ruggie sought a one-year extension in order to submit "views and recommendations," as requested by the Council. In 2007, the Human Rights Council renewed Ruggie's mandate for an additional year, inviting him to submit recommendations.

He returned in June 2008 with only one recommendation – that the Council endorse a conceptual framework, explaining the responsibility of corporations to respect human rights: the Protect, Respect and Remedy Framework ("the Framework").[11] The Council did so unanimously.

The Framework

As I outlined in Chapter 1, the Framework comprises three pillars:

1   the State duty to protect against human rights abuses by third parties – including business enterprises – through appropriate policies, regulation, and adjudication;

2   the corporate responsibility to respect human rights, which means that business enterprises should act with due diligence to avoid infringing on the rights of others and to address the adverse impacts with which they are involved; and

3   the need for victims to have greater access to effective remedy, both judicial and non-judicial, including State-based and non-State-based mechanisms.

The Council endorsed the Framework and, at the same time, renewed Professor Ruggie's mandate for a final three-year period until June 2011, asking him to "operationalize" the Framework. The culmination of this final work phase is the Guiding Principles, which provide practical recommendations for the Framework's implementation.

Table 5.1 Phases of Professor Ruggie's work

Phase One	2005–2007	Initially appointed for two years, Professor Ruggie was asked to "identify and clarify" existing standards and practices for corporate responsibility and accountability with regard to human rights.
Phase Two	2007–2008	The Council renewed Ruggie's mandate for an additional year in 2007, inviting him to submit recommendations. In June 2008, Professor Ruggie made only one recommendation: that the Human Rights Council support the "Protect, Respect and Remedy" Framework for managing business and human rights challenges which he had developed over the past three years.
Phase Three	2008–2011	The Council unanimously welcomed the Framework through resolution 8/7 and extended Ruggie's mandate for a final three years (until June 2011) to "operationalize" the Framework. The result was the UN Guiding Principles.

The UN Guiding Principles

The Guiding Principles were unanimously endorsed by the UN Human Rights Council on 16 June 2011.

At the time, Professor Ruggie stated, "The Council's endorsement establishes the Guiding Principles as the authoritative global reference point for business and human rights" and that "They will also provide civil society, investors and others the tools to measure real progress in the daily lives of people."[12]

There are 31 Guiding Principles. As a voluntary, multi-stakeholder initiative, they are not legally binding. Nonetheless, they apply to *all* corporations.

To better understand the Guiding Principles, it is useful to outline some of their most important features. The Guiding Principles:

1   apply to all States and all companies, irrespective of the company's size, sector, location, ownership or structure, but are completely voluntary in nature;
2   acknowledge the capacity of business to impact on all internationally recognised human rights;
3   clarify that human rights cannot be offset. That is, doing good in one place cannot compensate for doing harm elsewhere;
4   require the meaningful engagement of all sectors in respecting human rights; and
5   do not create any new legal obligations for States or business. Likewise, they do not undermine or limit any existing legal obligations.[13]

The remainder of this book will address the implications of human rights for business, outlining some of the most salient legal and non-legal impacts.

From a practical perspective, it will also provide some crucial steps – based on the Guiding Principles and other leading multi-stakeholder initiatives – that corporations can take to proactively manage their risks and adverse impacts in this area.

Notes

1 Development and International Economic Cooperation: Transnational Corporations, UN Doc. E/1 990/94; Draft United Nations Code of Conduct on Transnational Corporations, May 1983, 23 ILM 626 (1984).
2 Draft UN Norms on the Responsibility of Transnational Corporations and other Business Enterprises with Regard to Human Rights, (2003) UN Doc E/CN.4/Sub.2/2003/12/Rev.2.
3 Weissbrodt, D. and Kruger, M. "Norms on the responsibilities of transnational corporations and other business enterprises with regards to human rights." *American Journal of International Law*, vol. 97, no. 901, 2003, p. 913.
4 As above, note 2, at A.[1], p. 4.
5 Cited by Bader, C. in *Evolution of a Corporate Idealist: When Girl Meets Oil*, Bibliomotion, 2014, p. 112.
6 Commission on Human Rights, Decision 2004/116, "Responsibilities of transnational corporations and related business enterprises with regard to human rights," 20 April 2004.
7 Commission on Human Rights, Human Rights Resolution 2005/69, "Human rights and transnational corporations and other business enterprises," 20 April 2005.
8 Commission on Human Rights, Resolution 2005/69, 20 April 2005.
9 Ruggie, J. "Business and human rights: Mapping international standards of responsibility and accountability for corporate acts," A/HRC/4/035, 9 February 2007.
10 As above at para 44.
11 Ruggie, J. "Protect, respect and remedy: A framework for business and human rights," A/HRC/8/5, 7 April 2008.
12 News Release, Office of the High Commissioner on Human Rights, 16 June 2011.
13 Newton, A. "Any volunteers? Challenges and opportunities for corporations implementing the responsibility to respect human rights." *Australian Journal of Corporate Law*, vol. 28, 2013, p. 74.

Part III

The implications of human rights for business

Part III of the book analyses the implications of human rights for business – from both a legal and non-legal perspective. Given the fluid and rapidly evolving nature of the business and human rights field, business's obligations (and our understanding of them) are constantly changing. This demands that corporations take a proactive and agile approach in managing these issues.

Following a general overview of the legal and non-legal implications of human rights for business, Chapters 8 and 9 analyse two areas of particular challenge in more detail: combatting modern slavery in business supply chains and addressing sexual harassment and discrimination in corporate culture.

The implications of human rights for business

Chapter 6

Legal implications

First and foremost, it must be underlined that human rights are a *legal* issue for business.

As this chapter outlines, corporations have a range of obligations relating to human rights under both international and domestic legal systems. As understanding and awareness of these obligations grows, it is likely there will be a paradigm shift in the conceptualisation of human rights as a substantive legal issue for business.

International law

As outlined in Chapter 1, the international human rights framework principally governs States, not individuals or corporate actors. Individuals and corporations are indirectly impacted when States' obligations under international human rights treaties are incorporated in domestic law.

However, in contrast to this general principle, there are certain provisions under international criminal law regarding human rights that *do* apply directly to private actors. Like the *Universal Declaration of Human Rights* ("UDHR"), the origin of these laws can be traced to the post-Second World War context.

In 1945, following the war, the Allies (the United States, the Soviet Union, the United Kingdom, and France) decided to try individual Nazis before the International Military Tribunal at Nuremberg in Germany for violations of international law.

As agreed by the Allies, certain acts constituted crimes within the Tribunal's jurisdiction for which there would be individual responsibility.[1] These included: crimes against peace, war crimes, and crimes against humanity.

In his book *An Introduction to International Law*, Mark W. Janis clarified the rationale behind the Tribunal:

> The Nuremberg Trial was meant to establish plainly and forcefully that the rules of public international law should and do apply to individuals. As the Nuremberg Tribunal held, "[c]rimes against international law are committed by men, not by abstract entities, and only by punishing individuals who commit such crimes can the provisions of international law be enforced." Nuremberg was also intended to demonstrate that the protection of human rights was too important a matter to be left entirely to states.[2]

Following the Nuremburg trials, there were a series of prosecutions brought against German industrialists from various companies, such as IG Farben and Krupp, who were either directly or indirectly involved in the atrocities committed by the Nazis. In each case it was company officers, rather than the company itself, who were prosecuted.

Despite the significant achievements of the Nuremberg Tribunal, establishing individual responsibility for egregious violations of human rights, it was not until 1998 that a permanent, universal international criminal court was agreed to, under the *Rome Statute*.[3] The statute entered into force in 2002, establishing a permanent forum in which to hold individuals directly accountable for their international crimes.

This leads us to the crucial question: can corporations and their officers also be held responsible for egregious human rights violations and prosecuted before the International Criminal Court ("ICC")?

In short, the answer is no and yes. While corporations themselves *cannot* be prosecuted as juridical persons under the Rome Statute of the ICC, corporate officers responsible for their company's criminal conduct *can be* investigated and prosecuted. This is because the *Rome Statute* confers personal jurisdiction only over natural persons, particularly if he or she is a national of a State party to the *Rome Statute*.

For corporate officers (including company directors), responsibility under international criminal law can arise in several ways. These include:

- directly committing a crime;
- aiding and abetting (or otherwise being complicit in) a crime; or
- engaging in a "common purpose" or in a "joint criminal exercise."

The distinctions between direct and indirect violations by corporate officers under international law are complex and multifaceted.

Various international criminal tribunals have used the concept of "aiding and abetting" or otherwise assisting in the commission of a crime. The elements of this crime require: an act by the principal; practical assistance, encouragement, or moral support by the accessory; a substantial effect on the perpetration of the crime; and knowledge that the accessory's acts or omissions would assist the commission of the crime. However, there does not need to be a common purpose or plan.[4]

Meanwhile, the concept of engaging in a "common purpose" or a "joint criminal exercise" is generally understood to involve: two or more persons who make a significant contribution to the relevant crime, and who possess the intent to commit the crime.

Professor David Scheffer, who led the United States' delegation in the UN talks creating the ICC, has clarified the risks posed by ICC jurisdiction to corporate officers. He has stated:

> If it were better understood as a risk in corporate circles, the potential exposure of corporate officers to ICC jurisdiction could significantly influence the conduct of multinational

corporations in situations of atrocity crimes under investigation by the Prosecutor. But that exercise needs to begin in university instruction and graduate business schools where the future leaders of multinational corporations are educated and trained.[5]

It is possible that one day the *Rome Statute* will be amended to also cover juridical persons, that is, corporate actors. For this to happen, there would need to be widespread support among States party to the treaty. For those States with economies reliant on its multinational corporations (either as home States or host States), it is highly unlikely that they would support changes that would expose their corporations to criminal liability before the ICC.[6] Accordingly, at this stage, it seems probable that the risks of prosecution for liability under international criminal law will remain with corporate officers.

Beyond the ICC statute, individuals can also be held responsible for international crimes under customary international law and, more specifically, under *jus cogens*. In short, customary law is evidence of general practice of States that is accepted as law. Supporting evidence of it can come from various sources, including a State's laws and judicial decisions, and from public statements and published materials. Customary law is binding on all States, unless a State specifically and persistently objects to it.

In contrast, *jus cogens* are pre-emptory and fundamental norms of international law from which *no* State can derogate; that is, whether a State consents or not is irrelevant. It is generally accepted that the following acts are prohibited under *jus cogens*: the use of force; genocide; slavery; gross violations of the right of people to self-determination; racial discrimination; and torture.[7] These standards might be extended to corporations as legal persons, or at least to corporate officers.

Domestic law

When a nation State signs and ratifies an international human rights treaty, it assumes international obligations. Under international law, it is then responsible for bringing its domestic laws into conformity with its international commitments.

Standard practice for incorporating international treaty obligations within domestic law varies from State to State. In some States – including the United Kingdom and other Commonwealth countries – treaty obligations need to be incorporated (or implemented) domestically through the enactment of legislation. In other States – including the United States, France, and many Latin American countries – ratified treaties automatically become part of domestic law, by the mere process of their ratification. In simple terms, this is how international human rights law becomes domestic law impacting individuals and corporations in the home State.

Notably, Virginia Leary has observed that: "In states with the system of automatic incorporation, legislative consent by at least one house of the legislature is generally required before the executive may ratify treaties."[8] In this way, it seems that the two methods described above may not be so far apart after all, as legislative assent to the obligations is obtained at either an earlier or later stage of the process.

Generally, most countries do seek to observe their international human rights law obligations. Nevertheless, in her 2002 article in *The Yale Law Journal*, the legal scholar Oona Hathaway stated that, "although the practices of countries that have ratified human rights treaties are generally better than those of countries that have not, noncompliance with treaty obligations appears common."[9]

With this background in mind, we now turn to consider the interconnections between human rights and corporate law in domestic legal systems. The Corporate Law Project was initiated by Professor Ruggie as part of his UN mandate.[10] It considered whether and how corporate and securities law in over 40 jurisdictions encourages companies to respect human rights. It examined and compared the different ways that States regulate corporations, notwithstanding their different legal, political, social, and economic contexts.

The Project concluded that:

Predictably, these states have varied policies, laws and processes in place. But there are important similarities too, not
least regarding the question this project set out to explore –
the extent to which corporate and securities law encourages
companies to respect human rights. Put simply, where human
rights impacts may harm the company's short or long-term
interests if they are not adequately identified, managed and
reported, companies and their officers may risk non-
compliance with a variety of rules promoting corporate governance, risk management and market safeguards. And even
where the company itself is not at risk, several states recog-
nize through their corporate and securities laws that responsible corporate practice should not entail negative social or
environmental consequences, including for human rights.[11]

In other words, according to the Corporate Law Project, in most
jurisdictions corporations have a limited obligation to consider the
social and environmental impacts of their activities. This obligation
usually derives from their financial reporting obligations: to report
all activity that might have a material impact on the company.

For example, in Australia, under the Australian Stock
Exchange's Corporate Governance Principles and Recommendations, a publicly listed company must disclose whether it has any
material economic, environmental, and social sustainability risks
and, if it does, how it manages (or intends to manage) those
risks.[12] If the company chooses not to report on these risks, it is
required to explain why it has chosen not to do so.

Nonetheless, confusion and ambiguity remain about what
companies are *required* to do in relation to human rights, and
even what they are *permitted* to do within the scope of their
obligations to shareholders. In many jurisdictions, legislation is
increasingly emerging that specifically addresses human rights
concerns as they relate to business. In many instances, this is providing much-needed clarity for corporations seeking to understand their responsibilities in this area.

Another difficulty identified by the Corporate Law Project is
the limited (to non-existent) coordination between corporate

regulators and government agencies tasked with implementing human rights obligations. As a result, companies and their officers appear to get little, if any, guidance on how best to oversee their company's respect for human rights.

Legislation addressing business's responsibility to respect human rights

Fortunately, in many jurisdictions, legislation is now being enacted (or existing legislation is being repurposed) to address aspects of corporations' responsibility to respect human rights. It appears that many businesses welcome legislation that clarifies their responsibilities for human rights. Indeed, in their 2011 joint statement welcoming the Guiding Principles, the international organisations representing global business emphasised the importance of States playing a strong role:

> [o]nly States have the ability to develop a positive national position on human rights that can set the tone and direction for all other actors in their countries. The respective obligations of States and enterprises should be seen as mutually supportive and intrinsically linked, particularly since the ability of companies to respect human rights can be directly affected by the actions of States.[13]

The examples below are far from exhaustive but are provided to illustrate the kinds of approaches different legislatures around the world are taking to business and human rights.

• United States of America

i Dodd–Frank Wall Street Reform and Consumer Protection Act 2010 (US)

This Act (often referred to as "Dodd–Frank") was enacted by President Obama in the wake of the global financial crisis. It introduced significant and widespread changes to financial regulation in the United States, impacting almost every part of the financial services industry.

Among Dodd–Frank's many provisions is Section 1502. This requires regulated entities to disclose to the Securities and Exchange Commission ("SEC") whether any of their products contain conflict minerals originating from the Democratic Republic of the Congo ("DRC"). Where products do contain DRC conflict minerals, public companies must submit a report to the SEC disclosing the source and chain of custody of the minerals.[14]

Section 1502 was intended to address Congress's concern that:

> the exploitation and trade of conflict minerals originating in the Democratic Republic of the Congo is helping to finance conflict characterized by extreme levels of violence in the eastern Democratic Republic of the Congo, particularly sexual and gender-based violence, and contributing to an emergency humanitarian situation therein.[15]

In this context, it is important to note the Republican-sponsored Financial CHOICE Bill, which was passed by the US House of Representatives in June 2017. If enacted, it would reverse much of the *Dodd–Frank Act*, including Section 1502, relating to conflict minerals. It remains to be seen whether the legislation will pass the Senate.

As expert commentators have written, it is likely that the Senate minority will attempt to block the bill by filibuster. Lawyer Dynda A. Thomas has commented, "Because there seems to be near unanimous support for the conflict minerals rule by Democrats, it is possible that a deal could be proposed to keep Section 1502 in exchange for votes from Senate Democrats on the overall measure."[16]

Accordingly, despite the legislative action underway to repeal Section 1502, it is quite possible that the conflict minerals provisions will remain in place, either in their current form or an amended form.

ii Alien Tort Claims Act 1789 (US)[17]

The *Alien Tort Claims Act 1789* ("ATCA") has existed since 1789 but was only resurrected in the 1980s by foreign nationals seeking remedies in US courts for human rights violations occurring outside the US. Despite recent court decisions curtailing the strength and reach of the ATCA, it remains important for human rights litigation both in the US and internationally.

In the landmark 1980 decision in *Filártiga* v. *Peña-Irala*, the US Court of Appeals for the Second Circuit established that US federal courts had jurisdiction to hear tort claims involving a violation of public international law (the law of nations) or a treaty of the US involving non-US citizens committed outside the US.[18] In the Filártiga case itself, the Court found for the family of Joelito Filártiga, a Paraguayan citizen, who was kidnapped and tortured to death in Paraguay by Américo Norberto Peña-Irala, the inspector general of police in Asunción.

However, the efficacy of the ATCA to provide redress for victims of corporate human rights violations was called into question by the US Supreme Court in its 2013 decision in *Kiobel* v. *Royal Dutch Petroleum Co.* The plaintiffs were citizens of Nigeria who alleged that Dutch, British, and Nigerian oil-exploration corporations aided and abetted the Nigerian Government in the 1990s to commit violations of customary international law.

In *Kiobel*, the US Supreme Court held that there is a presumption *against* the extraterritorial application of US laws, including the ATCA. However, this presumption can be displaced when claims "touch and concern the territory of the United States … with sufficient force."[19]

Subsequently, in April 2018, the US Supreme Court ruled (by a vote of five to four) in *Jesner* v. *Arab Bank* that foreign corporations *cannot* be sued in US courts for complicity in human rights abuses abroad.[20] The case was brought by victims of terrorist attacks that occurred over a ten-year period in Israel, the West Bank, and Gaza. The victims alleged that Arab Bank (a Jordanian organisation) kept accounts for known terrorists, accepted donations that it knew would fund terrorism, and distributed millions of dollars to families of suicide bombers. The relevant connection of Arab Bank with the US was its branch located in New York.

In her dissenting opinion, Justice Sonia Sotomayor criticised the majority decision, stating that they had "used a sledgehammer to crack a nut." That is, it was open to the majority to find that the claim's connection with the US (transactions being processed in the bank's New York branch) was too tangential to meet the "touch and concern" test set out in *Kiobel*. Instead, by holding that foreign corporations cannot be sued in the US under the ATCA in any circumstance, the implications of their ruling are much broader.

As a result of *Jesner*, even if a sufficient connection with the US can be proven, foreign corporations can no longer be sued under the ATCA for egregious human rights violations. However, given the facts of this case, the Court did *not* consider whether an alien can sue a US corporation under the ATCA. Likewise, individual corporate officers might still be sued under *Jesner*. This means that the door is still open in the US for victims to bring tort cases for corporate violations of their human rights.

iii Transparency in Supply Chains Act 2010 (US)

The *Transparency in Supply Chains Act 2010* ("TSCA") came into effect in California in 2012. It requires any retailer or manufacturer doing business in California with an annual global turnover of more than US$100 million to publicly disclose their anti-trafficking and anti-slavery policies.

The legislation requires that companies disclose on their website their initiatives to eliminate slavery and human trafficking from their direct supply chain for goods sold.

A series of class action lawsuits has been brought under the TSCA against Hershey's, Mars, and Nestlé. Finding in favour of the companies, the Court ruled that the law requires companies to report on their efforts to prevent slavery and human trafficking in their supply chains; not to disclose individual instances where they may have encountered it, to change their anti-trafficking policies or to implement policies if none are in place.[21]

US federal legislation is also in the pipeline, with the Business Supply Chain Transparency on Trafficking and Slavery Bill 2015 currently before the House Committee on Financial Services.[22] If enacted, it will require companies to make similar disclosures to those required under the TSCA.

• *United Kingdom*

The United Kingdom's *Modern Slavery Act 2015* ("MSA") was modelled on California's TSCA and came into effect in October 2015.

Under the MSA, every company carrying on business in the UK with an annual global turnover of £36 million or more must publish a slavery and human trafficking statement each year, outlining the steps taken to ensure slavery and trafficking are not occurring in their supply chain. Alternatively, under Section 54 of the MSA, if a company chooses not to publish a statement, it may simply state that it has taken no such steps.

Notably, like the TSCA, the MSA does not require companies to take action to combat slavery, but companies are obliged to publicly disclose if they are not taking such steps.

Should companies fail to comply with their obligations under the MSA, civil proceedings for an injunction can be brought against them by the UK secretary of state. The fact that companies are not liable for monetary or criminal penalties for non-compliance has been criticised by various commentators who consider that the MSA lacks teeth. Modern slavery in corporate supply chains is discussed in more detail in Chapter 8.

• *France*

In February 2017, the French Parliament passed a duty of vigilance law requiring French companies to take serious human rights challenges into account. Its title translates to "the law about the duty of due diligence of parent companies and main contractors."[23]

The law imposes a duty of care with three elements: elaboration, disclosure, and effective implementation of a "vigilance plan." The vigilance plan requires that the company take "reasonable vigilance measures to adequately identify risks and prevent serious violations of human rights and fundamental freedoms, risks and serious harms to health and safety and the environment."[24]

The law encompasses all French companies (and their subsidiaries) that have more than 5,000 employees domestically, or more than 10,000 employees worldwide.

• *Australia*

In June 2018, New South Wales ("NSW") became the first Australian State to introduce modern slavery legislation when a private member's bill passed both houses of Parliament with bipartisan support.[25]

Under the NSW *Modern Slavery Act*, commercial organisations with at least one employee in NSW, and with a total annual turnover of at least A\$50 million, are required to publish an annual modern slavery statement. Companies not complying with the legislation face penalties of up to 10,000 penalty units or the equivalent of A\$1.1 million. The NSW Act also provides for an independent anti-slavery commissioner.

At the federal level, the *Modern Slavery Act* commenced in Australia on 1 January 2019. The Act requires businesses with global consolidated revenue of A\$100 million or more to report annually on the risks of modern slavery in their operations and supply chains, and the action they have taken to assess and address those risks, and the effectiveness of their response.

Three important differences are worth noting between the NSW and federal Modern Slavery Acts in Australia. First, in contrast to the NSW Act, the federal *Modern Slavery Act* does not include penalties for non-compliance. Second, the federal Act does not provide for an independent oversight mechanism, such as an anti-slavery commissioner. And, third, the lower revenue reporting threshold of A\$50 million in NSW means that smaller entities will be captured by that legislation.

To avoid duplication in reporting, the NSW Act provides that the reporting requirement will not apply to commercial organisations which report under a prescribed equivalent federal or state law.

The legislation follows a federal inquiry into modern slavery legislation in 2017. Australia's Attorney-General requested Parliament's Joint Standing Committee on Foreign Affairs, Defence and Trade to inquire into and report on establishing a Modern Slavery Act in Australia. The Committee's Final Report, *Hidden in Plain Sight*, was published in December 2017.[26] Among its 49 recommendations, the Committee recommended that the Australian Government introduce a Modern Slavery Act drawing on, but strengthening, the UK *Modern Slavery Act 2015*. The Committee also recommended that the proposed Act should establish an independent anti-slavery commissioner and supply chain reporting requirements for entities operating in Australia.

From the perspective of many civil society groups and anti-slavery campaigners, the legislation (in particular, the federal Act) could have gone further. However, the implications of both Acts for business are significant, and it is hoped that they will play an important role in combatting modern slavery.

This section has sought to provide a snapshot in time of legislation from around the world relating to business and human rights. The examples are likely to multiply as more States create National Action Plans ("NAPs") to implement the UN Guiding Principles. Currently, as of publication, 22 States have a NAP in place, with dozens more States having committed to developing one.[27] It demonstrates the importance of treating human rights as a legal issue for business that must be managed proactively and continuously. There are many more examples from a panoply of jurisdictions that may be relevant for a company to consider, depending on the substantive area concerned and the specific challenges involved. In each case, a company should seek legal advice to ensure its human rights risks and challenges are managed appropriately.

Notes

1 *Agreement for the Prosecution and Punishment of the Major War Criminals of the European Axis*, art. 6, 59 Stat. 1544, 1547–1548.
2 Janis, Mark W. *An Introduction to International Law*, 4th ed., Aspen, 2003, p. 259.
3 On 17 July 1998 more than 100 countries (not including the United States) agreed on the *Rome Treaty* to create a permanent international criminal court.
4 See generally: Ventura, Manuel J., "Aiding and abetting" (16 April 2018). de Hemptinne, Jérôme, Roth, Robert, and van Sliedregt, Elies (eds), *Modes of Liability in International Criminal Law*, Cambridge University Press, 2018 (Forthcoming). Accessed on 11 September 2018: https://papers.ssrn.com/sol3/papers.cfm?abstract_id=3160960.
5 Scheffer, David. "Corporate liability under the Rome Statute." *Harvard International Law Journal*, 7 July 2016. Accessed on 22 July 2018: www.harvardilj.org/2016/07/corporate-liability-under-the-rome-statute.
6 As above.
7 Alston, Philip and Goodman, Ryan. *International Human Rights*, Oxford University Press, 2013, p. 78.
8 Leary, Virginia. *International Labour Conventions and National Law*, Springer, 1982.
9 Hathaway, Oona A. "Do human rights treaties make a difference?" Faculty Scholarship Series. Paper 839, 2002, p. 1940: http://digital commons.law.yale.edu/fss_papers/839.
10 Ruggie, J. *Corporate Law Project: Overarching Trends and Observations*, July 2010. Accessed on 23 July 2018: www.business-humanrights.org/sites/default/files/reports-and-materials/Ruggie-corporate-law-project-Jul-2010.pdf.
11 As above.
12 Australian Stock Exchange. *Corporate Governance Principles and Recommendations*, 3rd ed., 2014, Recommendation 7.4. Accessed on 23 July, 2018: www.asx.com.au/documents/asx-compliance/cgc-principles-and-recommendations-3rd-edn.pdf.
13 International Chamber of Commerce, the International Organisation of Employers, and the Business and Industry Advisory Committee (BIAC) to the OECD. *Joint Statement on Business & Human Rights to the United Nations Human Rights Council*, 30 May 2011.

Accessed on 23 July 2018: https://cdn.iccwbo.org/content/uploads/sites/3/2011/05/Joint-Statement-on-Business-Human-Rights-to-the-United-Nations-Human-Rights-Council.pdf.

14 The issue of conflict minerals in the electronics industry is discussed in more detail in Chapter 17.

15 *Dodd–Frank Wall Street Reform and Consumer Protection Act 2010* (US), p. 838.

16 Thomas, Dynda A. "Conflict minerals rule – Will it stay or will it go?" Squire Patton Boggs website. Accessed on 6 July 2018: www.conflictmineralslaw.com/2017/05/11/conflict-minerals-rule-will-it-stay-or-will-it-go.

17 The text of the ATCA states: "The district courts shall have original jurisdiction of any civil action by an alien for a tort only, committed in violation of the law of nations or a treaty of the United States."

18 *Filártiga* v. *Peña-Irala*, 630 F.2d 876 (2d Cir. 1980).

19 *Kiobel* v. *Royal Dutch Petroleum Co.*, 569 U.S. (2013), Slip Opinion at 16.

20 *Jesner* v. *Arab Bank PLC*, 584 U.S. (2018).

21 See: Newton, A. "Analysis: is modern slavery legislation up to the challenge?" *Ethical Corporation*, 18 November 2016. Accessed on 19 June: www.ethicalcorp.com/analysis-modern-slavery-legislation-challenge.

22 Business Supply Chain Transparency on Trafficking and Slavery Bill 2015. Accessed on 19 June: www.congress.gov/bill/114th-congress/house-bill/3226/text.

23 In French, the Act is entitled: "*Loi relative au devoir de vigilance des sociétés mères et des entrprises donneuses d'ordre.*"

24 Cossart, S., Chaplier, J., and Beau De Lomenie, T. "Developments in the field: The French law on duty of care: A historic step towards making globalization work for all." *Business and Human Rights Journal*, vol. 2, 2017, pp. 317–323, p. 320.

25 Modern Slavery Bill, Parliament of New South Wales. Accessed on 4 July 2018: www.parliament.nsw.gov.au/bills/Pages/bill-details.aspx?pk=3488.

26 *Hidden in Plain Sight*, Final Report, Inquiry into establishing a Modern Slavery Act in Australia, 2017. Accessed on 19 June 2018: www.aph.gov.au/Parliamentary_Business/Committees/Joint/Foreign_Affairs_Defence_and_Trade/ModernSlavery/Final_report.

27 Business and Human Rights Resource Centre, National Action Plans. Accessed on 10 December 2018: www.business-humanrights.org/en/un-guiding-principles/implementation-tools-examples/implementation-by-governments/by-type-of-initiative/national-action-plans.

Chapter 7

Non-legal obligations and their implications

Multi-stakeholder initiatives

In addition to corporations' legal obligations, they also face a suite of non-legal, voluntary obligations and standards relating to their social and environmental impacts.

These non-legal obligations generally come in the form of international frameworks or multi-stakeholder initiatives. Like corporations' legal obligations, multi-stakeholder initiatives are essential for preventing and addressing business's potential adverse impacts on human rights.

There are various types of multi-stakeholder initiatives including industry-specific and regional initiatives. They may be State-sponsored (such as the OECD Guidelines for Multinational Enterprises) or initiated by industry (such as the Electronics Industry Citizenship Coalition). Consideration of a corporation's industry, combined with the particular risks and challenges it faces, will inform which multi-stakeholder initiative (or initiatives) it chooses to follow.

Given the vast array of multi-stakeholder initiatives, it is understandable that corporate executives can sometimes feel overwhelmed by the process of selecting and implementing the best initiative/s for their business. Once implemented, many initiatives require regular and ongoing reporting from the corporation to maintain favourable status. If not carefully managed by an executive with the necessary skills and experience, meeting these obligations can also become overwhelming.

For example, the UN Global Compact, the world's largest multi-stakeholder initiative, requires participants to lodge an annual communication on progress (CoP). The CoP is a form of non-financial reporting that includes information on the actions a company has taken (or plans to take) to implement the ten principles set out in the UN Global Compact, and a measurement of outcomes achieved.

Table 7.1 sets out some of the most important multi-stakeholder initiatives relating to business and human rights, arranged by industry. For more examples and the full text of initiatives, see the Business and Human Rights Resource Centre's website.[1]

Given the specialised nature of many multi-stakeholder initiatives, each brings its own benefits and unique insights to a company's activities and supply chain. However, since 2011, in the realm of business and human rights, much of the focus has coalesced around the UN Guiding Principles. Other multi-stakeholder initiatives – such as the OECD Guidelines, the Equator Principles, and the International Finance Corporation's Performance Standards on Environmental and Social Sustainability – have been updated to explicitly incorporate the Guiding Principles' basic precepts.

Reputational risk

Benjamin Franklin reportedly said, "It takes many good deeds to build a good reputation, and only one bad one to lose it." This statement definitely applies in the context of business's management of their adverse impacts on human rights.

To the extent that a company's overall reputation is a function of its reputation among its various stakeholders, its participation in and with multi-stakeholder initiatives is crucial.

Further, as multi-stakeholder initiatives and international frameworks have become more established and normative for business, the implications for corporations choosing not to

Table 7.1 Key multi-stakeholder initiatives on business and human rights

General initiatives	Established	Areas covered/scope
UN Guiding Principles on Business and Human Rights	2011	Applies to all corporations and all industries. Articulates States' duty to protect and the corporate responsibility to respect human rights. Also highlights the need for greater access to remedy.
UN Global Compact	2005	Sets out ten principles incorporating: human rights, labour, the environment, and anti-corruption.
OECD Guidelines for Multinational Enterprises	1976 (but amended numerous times)	Addresses various aspects of responsible business including: human rights, employment, bribery, the environment, information disclosure, consumer interests, science and technology, competition, and taxation.
ISO Standards 26000 – Social responsibility	2010	Provides guidance on social responsibility for business, including ethics and transparency.
Global Reporting Initiative	1997	Global initiative that publishes a corporate social responsibility reporting framework for companies. The framework sets out indicators that brands can use to measure and report their economic, environmental and social performance.

Table 7.1 Continued

Industry-specific initiatives	Established	Areas covered/scope
Extractives Extractive Industries Transparency Initiative	2003	The global standard to promote the open and accountable management of oil, gas, and mineral resources. Premised on greater transparency being achieved by companies disclosing the sum they pay and States disclosing the sum they receive.
Kimberley Process	2003	International certification scheme imposing extensive requirements on its members to enable rough diamonds to be certified as "conflict free."
Voluntary Principles on Security and Human Rights	2000	Guidance on maintaining the safety and security of an extraction site, while respecting human rights.
Banking and finance Equator Principles	2003	Risk management framework used by financial institutions for determining, assessing and managing environmental and social risks in project finance.
Thun Group of Banks	2013	Group of banks formed to better understand the implications of the UN Guiding Principles for the banking sector.

continued

Table 7.1 Continued

Industry-specific initiatives	Established	Areas covered/scope
Apparel		
Fair Wear Foundation	1999	International verification initiative focusing on labour standards in the garment sector. Verifies that its member companies implement its Code of Labor Practices in their supply chains through process audits and verification.
Accord on Fire and Building Safety in Bangladesh	2013	Independent, legally binding agreement between global brands, retailers, and trade unions designed to build a safe and healthy Bangladeshi ready-made garment industry.
Better Cotton Initiative	2009	Group comprised of international brands and NGOs that aims to improve cotton-growing conditions through a product certification programme, including social and environmental indicators.
Information technology		
Electronics Industry Citizenship Coalition	2004	Through the application of a shared standard, works to create better social, economic, and environmental outcomes for all involved in electronics and ICT supply chains.

implement them, or implementing them poorly, have grown. While there may not be any *legal* implications for a corporation failing to implement multi-stakeholder initiatives relevant to their enterprise, the implications for a corporation's reputation can be significant.

For example, the UN Guiding Principles, broadly considered to be the international gold standard in the field of business and human rights, are being implemented by almost all major corporations with a leading practice in social sustainability or corporate responsibility. Those corporations not engaged with the Guiding Principles are likely to fall into the laggard category and to see their reputations suffer, even if they may in other respects have good practices throughout their operations.

Reputation risk management is itself a burgeoning field of scholarship and practice. Andrea Bonime-Blanc, the CEO of GEC Risk Advisory[2] and the author of *The Reputation Risk Handbook: Surviving and Thriving in an Age of Hyper-Transparency*, has developed a framework and a range of tools for corporations seeking to manage risk and reputation directly.[3]

In an interview with FAIR Institute, Dr Bonime-Blanc cites an example of the reputational and financial cost poor reputational risk management can exact on a company. She said:

> Reputation loss can kill a company; just look at the Weinstein Co, once a leading independent film studio, that went broke after 60+ actresses accused Harvey Weinstein of sexual harassment and assault. The resulting lawsuits and cancelled deals made the company unsaleable even after Weinstein exited. Reputation-generated losses exceeded the total value of the company, so to speak.[4]

Financial risk

Like reputational impacts, the financial implications of a company's failure to address its adverse impacts on human rights can also be significant.

Reputational losses invariably lead to financial losses. As in the example of the Weinstein Company above, enormous financial losses (greater even than the value of the company) can be directly traced to a loss in Harvey Weinstein's – and hence the company's – reputations.

However, beyond reputational issues, there are clearly other reasons why a company's adverse impacts on human rights can result in financial losses. Most notably, the costs to rectify damage, operational costs, and compensation to victims resulting from human rights violations can be extraordinarily high for a company attempting to address them.

For example, Samarco, and its co-owners, BHP and Vale, are facing a civil claim for 155 billion reals (approximately US$41.4 billion) for social, environmental, and economic compensation relating to the Samarco iron ore tailings dam failure in November 2015 in the Minas Gerais region. The dam collapse killed 19 people, injured many more, and destroyed the homes and livelihoods of hundreds of people in the region.

BP's costs in its 2010 Deepwater Horizon explosion and oil spill are another example of the massive financial implications flowing from a company's adverse impacts on human rights and the environment. Ultimately, clean-up of the oil spill and its resulting damage totalled around US$62 billion. The costs cover multiple comprehensive settlements with federal and state authorities, shareholders, property owners, and consumers.

Leaving aside the tragic human costs of the events above, which cannot be quantified in any meaningful way, the financial costs for the corporations involved were crippling. It begs the question: if this is the case for large corporations like BHP, Vale, and BP, how much more financially devastating would the impacts be for smaller or medium-sized companies if they were to be faced with a similar scenario?

Notes

1 Business and Human Rights Resource Centre, Principles. Accessed on 19 June: www.business-humanrights.org/en/principles.
2 The author notes her affiliation, as a specialist in business and human rights, with GEC Risk Advisory's team.
3 Bonime-Blanc, Andrea. *The Reputation Risk Handbook: Surviving and Thriving in an Age of Hyper-Transparency*, 1st ed., Routledge, 2014.
4 Copeland, Jeff B. "Measuring reputation loss (and gain) with Andrea Bonime-Blanc," FAIR Institute Blog, 1 March 2018. Accessed on 1 May 2018: www.fairinstitute.org/blog/measuring-reputation-loss-and-gain-with-andrea-bonime-blanc.

Chapter 8

Preventing modern slavery in corporate supply chains

In Chapter 6, I outlined some examples of legislation on modern slavery in various jurisdictions around the world including the US, the UK and Australia. Given the prevalence of slavery today and the potential for multinational companies' supply chains to be implicated (often unwittingly), this chapter provides a deeper analysis of this important issue.

With an estimated 40.3 million people living in slavery around the world,[1] and 90 per cent of these victims being exploited in the private economy,[2] it is no surprise that the pressure on companies to prevent and manage the risks of human rights violations in their supply chains is intensifying.

Recognising the severity of the threat posed by modern slavery, various parliaments around the world have responded with legislation specifically addressing it.

This chapter analyses the key provisions and effectiveness of two of the most critical pieces of legislation on this issue: California's *Transparency in Supply Chains Act 2010* ("TSCA") and the UK's *Modern Slavery Act 2015* ("MSA").

It also highlights new modern slavery legislation in Australia, passed by the Federal Parliament in late 2018 following a parliamentary inquiry into establishing a Modern Slavery Act.

Notably, US federal legislation is also in the pipeline, with the Business Supply Chain Transparency on Trafficking and Slavery Bill 2015 currently before the House Committee on Financial

Services.[3] If enacted, it will require companies to make similar disclosures to those required under the TSCA.

However, at this stage, it is unclear how effective all this legislation will be to combat the enormous challenge posed by slavery and human trafficking in complex, global supply chains that are often labyrinthine and dispersed in nature.

What does the legislation require? Who is affected?

Both the MSA and the TSCA require companies to report on the steps they have taken to eradicate slavery and human trafficking in their supply chains, or to disclose if they are not taking such steps. Notably, neither requires a company to report on the possibility of slave labour actually existing in its supply chain.

This was confirmed by a series of class action lawsuits brought in 2015 under the TSCA against Hershey's, Mars, and Nestlé. Finding in favour of the companies, the Court ruled that the law requires companies to report on their efforts to prevent slavery and human trafficking in their supply chains. However, they are not required to disclose individual instances where they may have encountered it, to change their anti-trafficking policies, or to implement policies if none are in place.

Which companies are affected?

The TSCA applies to any retail seller or manufacturer doing business in California that has an annual worldwide gross receipt of more than US$100 million. The MSA potentially covers any company supplying goods or services that operates in the UK and has an annual global turnover exceeding £36 million. Significantly, companies headquartered or registered outside California or the UK, respectively, may still have obligations under the legislation. While the TSCA affects about 3,200 companies, the MSA applies to approximately 12,000 UK and non-UK companies.

Table 8.1 Comparison of US and UK modern slavery legislation

Transparency in Supply Chains Act 2010 (US)	Modern Slavery Act 2015 (UK)
Applies to: retail sellers and manufacturers	Applies to: *all* sectors – commercial organisations supplying goods or services
US$100 million (annual worldwide receipts)	£36 million (annual global turnover)
Scope: "direct supply chain"	Scope: "in any of its supply chains" *and* "in any parts of its own business"
Frequency of reporting: does not specify how often statement is to be updated	Frequency of reporting: statement required each financial year
Companies covered: approx. 3,200	Companies covered: approx. 12,000

How effective are the Acts likely to be?

It is still early days, particularly for the MSA; statements are compulsory in relation to financial years ending on or after 31 March 2016. (The UK Government encourages reporting within six months of the financial year end.) Nonetheless, serious concerns have been raised about whether the MSA has real teeth. Section 54 of the Act says a company may simply state that it has taken no such steps if it chooses not to publish a statement under the MSA.

It is concerning that of those companies that have published statements so far many have failed to comply with the Act's requirements. According to Ergon Associates, which analysed more than 230 statements by companies, about 40 per cent have not been signed by a director and about a third cannot be accessed via a link easily found on the organisation's homepage (both of which are required under the MSA). Also, there is no monetary or criminal penalty for companies' non-compliance.

Instead, civil proceedings for an injunction can be brought against a company by the secretary of state.

The Business & Human Rights Resource Centre has created a registry of statements to benchmark companies' policies and practices. Currently it contains more than 4,500 statements.

Similarly, the TSCA has been criticised for lacking strength and transparency. It requires companies subject to it to disclose their efforts to eradicate slavery and human trafficking only in their direct supply chain. This obligation is more circumscribed than that under the MSA, and is likely to be a real deficiency given the dispersed and expansive nature of most modern supply chains.

Another criticism of the TSCA is that it does not specify how often a business is required to update its statement. Given the very fluid and dynamic nature of supply chains, this omission is problematic and is inconsistent with the well-accepted principle that human rights due diligence should be regular and ongoing. Further, it does not require that the names of the companies subject to it be made public.

In 2015, Know the Chain, a resource for businesses and investors to understand and address forced labour abuses in their supply chains, reported that only 31 per cent of the corporations required to comply with the TSCA had a disclosure statement available that complied with all the requirements of the Act.

Australian developments

The *Modern Slavery Act* commenced in Australia on 1 January 2019. The Act requires businesses with global consolidated revenue of A$100 million or more to report annually on the risks of modern slavery in their operations and supply chains, and the action they have taken to assess and address those risks, and the effectiveness of their response.

The Act requires that the statement be approved by the board of directors and signed by a director. The statements will be made publicly available on a central register maintained by the Federal Government.

In addition to the reporting requirements on entities with annual consolidated revenue of A$100 million or more, entities with employees in New South Wales ("NSW") will be obliged to report under the NSW Act if they have an annual turnover of between A$50 million and A$100 million.

Notably, the Australian Government has claimed that the *Modern Slavery Act* will achieve a "world first" by also publishing an annual statement covering Commonwealth Government procurement. The Assistant Minister for Home Affairs stated, "This underlines the Government's commitment to leading by example in the fight against modern slavery."[4]

While the legislation has been enthusiastically welcomed by many, it has been criticised for not including penalties for non-compliance and for lacking an independent oversight mechanism, such as an anti-slavery commissioner.

Notably, the Parliamentary Inquiry's Final Report into whether Australia should establish legislation to combat modern slavery, *Hidden in Plain Sight*, was tabled in December 2017. Among other things, it recommended both the establishment of an independent anti-slavery commissioner and penalties for non-reporting entities.[5]

While the *Modern Slavery Act* does not go as far as the Parliamentary Inquiry and many in civil society would have liked, it is nonetheless a good start.

What does this mean for business?

Human rights violations in corporate supply chains are an expanding area of legal and reputational risk that business should seek to manage proactively.

While the MSA and TSCA have been criticised for lacking real teeth, they nevertheless have focused public attention on corporate supply chains and, in many instances, have highlighted abuses that were previously hidden. It is hoped that the new Australian legislation will do likewise.

Businesses should identify areas of risk for slavery and human trafficking, implement effective and ongoing human rights due diligence processes and remedies, and seek continuously to improve their oversight and understanding of supply chain risks.

Notes

1 "Global findings," *The Global Slavery Index*, 2018. Accessed on 9 December 2018: www.globalslaveryindex.org/2018/findings/global-findings.
2 ILO. *Profits and Poverty: The Economics of Forced Labour*, 2014. Accessed on 8 June 2018: www.ilo.org/global/topics/forced-labour/publications/profits-of-forced-labour-2014/lang–en/index.htm.
3 Business Supply Chain Transparency on Trafficking and Slavery Bill 2015, Congress.Gov. Accessed on 25 July 2018: www.congress.gov/bill/114th-congress/house-bill/3226/text.
4 The Hon Alex Hawke MP, Assistant Minister for Home Affairs. "Government strengthens Australia's response to modern slavery," Thursday, 10 May 2018. Accessed on 8 June 2018: http://minister.homeaffairs.gov.au/alexhawke/Pages/modern-slavery.aspx.
5 Joint Standing Committee on Foreign Affairs, Defence and Trade. *Hidden in Plain Sight*, December 2017. Accessed on 8 June 2018: www.aph.gov.au/Parliamentary_Business/Committees/Joint/Foreign_Affairs_Defence_and_Trade/ModernSlavery/Final_report.

Chapter 9

Addressing sexual harassment and discrimination in corporate culture

International human rights law prohibits discrimination and violence against women, including sexual harassment. However, given its ongoing prevalence in many areas of women's lives – and particularly in the workplace – this is a critical issue for all businesses to address.

Some of the key instruments in international law include:

- The *Convention on the Elimination of All Forms of Discrimination Against Women* (CEDAW), which directs States to take appropriate measures to eliminate discrimination against women in all fields, specifically including equality under law, in governance and politics, the workplace, education, healthcare, and other areas of public and social life (Articles 7–16).[1]
- The *Declaration on the Elimination of Violence Against Women*, which defines violence against women to include sexual harassment. This is prohibited at work, in educational institutions, and elsewhere (Article 2(b)). The Declaration encourages the development of penal, civil, or other administrative sanctions, as well as preventative approaches to eliminate violence against women (Article 4(d–f)).[2]
- The ILO's *Discrimination (Employment and Occupation) Convention (No. 111) of 1958* prohibits sexual harassment as a form of sex discrimination.[3]

Many countries have implemented their international human rights obligations to combat violence and discrimination against women in their domestic legislation. In some cases, this has been done under anti-discrimination or human rights legislation; in other cases, it has been incorporated under a State's criminal law.

Growing awareness of sexual harassment

Recently, the movement to combat sexual harassment and discrimination in all its forms has accelerated around the world. Specifically, the MeToo and TimesUp Movements have shone the light of international scrutiny on corporate cultures that acquiesce in or enable harassment, discrimination, or other forms of violence against women.

In October 2017, the #MeToo hashtag went viral on social media in attempts to demonstrate the prevalence of sexual harassment and assault, particularly in the workplace. This followed Pulitzer Prize-winning reports by the *New York Times*[4] and the *New Yorker*[5] that the influential American film producer Harvey Weinstein was accused by dozens of women of rape and sexual assault, stretching over a period of more than 30 years. Subsequently, more than 70 women came forward with similar allegations against Weinstein.

On 25 May 2018, Weinstein was arrested and charged with rape and other offences. He has pleaded not guilty to all the charges against him, unequivocally and repeatedly denying that he has had non-consensual sex.[6] If convicted of the various charges, Weinstein faces a minimum of ten years' and a maximum of life imprisonment.

Weinstein enjoyed impunity for many years, despite the plethora of allegations against him and his widespread reputation in Hollywood as a womaniser. His "casting couch practices" were so notorious that, at the 85th Academy Awards in 2013, host Seth MacFarlane joked when announcing the Best Supporting Actress nominees: "Congratulations, you five ladies no longer have to pretend to be attracted to Harvey Weinstein."[7]

In addition to his enormous cachet as a celebrity film producer, it appears that Weinstein's seeming invulnerability may have also emanated, at least in part, from his support for leading Democrat politicians, including his claims of being friends with Bill and Hillary Clinton and Barack Obama. (Notably, in October 2017, Hillary Clinton and Barack and Michelle Obama denounced Weinstein's reported behaviour).

The *New Yorker* and *Times* articles claim that Weinstein's activities were enabled by various employees, associates, and agents who arranged his meetings with actresses often in hotel rooms and other private locations, and by lawyers and publicists who suppressed complaints with payments and threats.

The allegations against Weinstein and the public debates that ensued have acted as a tipping point and catalyst for women to share their experiences of sexual assault and harassment in all its forms. This has been termed the "Weinstein effect." It has triggered allegations of sexual harassment and/or assault against other powerful men around the world, and across a range of industries including business, politics, entertainment, technology, and sport.

Some other recent examples of high-profile sexual harassment and assault cases (both before and after the Weinstein allegations broke) are outlined below.

Investment banking

In a long-running case that has been ongoing since 2010, gender discrimination has been alleged against the global investment bank Goldman Sachs.[8] Specifically, the plaintiffs allege that Goldman Sachs has distributed the benefits of its success unequally by systematically favouring male associates and vice presidents at the expense of their female counterparts. The plaintiffs allege that this has occurred by:

- at most levels of its professional ranks, paying female professionals less than similarly situated males, despite them holding equivalent positions and performing the same or similar work;

- maintaining policies and practices for promoting its vice presidents that result in the disproportionate promotion of men over equally, or more, qualified women;
- evaluating employees' performance through systems lacking key safeguards to ensure fairness and proper implementation, resulting in the systematic undervaluation of female employees' performance; and
- allowing managers (the vast majority of whom are men) to assign responsibilities without accountability measures to ensure fairness, resulting in the most lucrative and promising opportunities going to male employees.[9]

The litigation is ongoing. At the time of writing, the most recent update on the case was issued in March 2018 by the United States District Court for the Southern District of New York.[10]

Politics

In May 2018, New York State Attorney General Eric Schneiderman was accused of physical assault by four women who claimed they were in a relationship with him at the time of the alleged violence. Two of the women alleged that Schneiderman threatened to kill them if they broke up with him. While Schneiderman has denied the allegations, he resigned his post while the claims were investigated.

This case is not just remarkable for the high public office held by Schneiderman. If the allegations against him are proven, it also underscores the intense hypocrisy between the public positions he has taken as a champion of women, and his actions in his personal life. As Attorney General, Schneiderman filed a civil rights suit against Harvey Weinstein and used his office to demand greater compensation for Weinstein's victims. He also introduced a bill that criminalised strangulation in New York State (given that several women accuse Schneiderman of violently strangling and attempting to choke them, this is particularly incredible). In addition, Schneiderman has strongly advocated for women's reproductive rights and, on 1 May 2018, was honoured as a "Champion of Choice" by the New York-based National Institute for Reproductive Health.[11]

Reporting on the claims, the *New Yorker* stated that:

> Over the past year, [two of his accusers] watched with admiration as other women spoke out about sexual misconduct. But, as [Mr] Schneiderman used the authority of his office to assume a major role in the #MeToo movement, their anguish and anger grew.[12]

Television

In 2016, a former anchor at the Fox News Channel, Gretchen Carlson, accused news chief Roger Ailes of harassment. Allegations of sexual harassment were also made against anchor Bill O'Reilly. In late 2017, Twenty-First Century Fox Inc. reached a $90 million settlement of shareholder claims arising from the sexual harassment scandal at its Fox News Channel.[13]

Similarly, at NBC, Matt Lauer, the former high-profile television personality and news anchor was terminated by the network following allegations of sexual harassment by a female employee at NBC.

The issue of sexual harassment appears to be similarly pervasive in Australia. In 2016, a survey by Women in Media (part of the Media Entertainment and Arts Alliance) found that, out of the 1,000 people surveyed, 48 per cent of women in media reported intimidation, abuse or sexual harassment in the workplace and a third were not confident in speaking up.[14]

Technology

In September 2015, a lawsuit (*Moussouris* v. *Microsoft Corporation*)[15] was filed against Microsoft Corporation alleging gender discrimination. Specifically, the complaint alleged systemic and pervasive discrimination against female employees in technical and engineering roles with respect to performance evaluations, pay, promotions, and other terms and conditions of employment.[16]

The plaintiffs claimed that sex discrimination is a result of the company's systematic policies and practices and lack of appropriate accountability mechanisms to ensure fairness. If the lawsuit is amended to a class action suit, it could add over 8,600 women to the list of plaintiffs. Previously, a separate lawsuit was filed against Microsoft, alleging pay gaps and pregnancy discrimination.[17]

Each of these examples provides a poignant reminder of the insidious nature of sexual harassment, abuse, and discrimination across all industries and sectors. Like the example of modern slavery in Chapter 8, it underscores the crucial importance of all businesses adopting proactive policies and practices to prevent sexual harassment, abuse and discrimination, and to provide victims with access to remedies when it does occur.

Backlash to the MeToo Movement

An alternative perspective on the MeToo Movement has emerged in France. In an open letter published in *Le Monde*, 99 prominent French women (including the well-known actress Catherine Deneuve) denounced the MeToo Movement as having gone too far and threatening women's sexual freedoms.[18]

In essence, the letter defended a "freedom to bother as indispensable to sexual freedom." It stated: "Rape is a crime. But trying to pick up someone, however persistently or clumsily, is not – nor is gallantry an attack of machismo."[19]

The French authors acknowledged the legitimacy of the international awakening to sexual violence and harassment sparked by the Weinstein scandal. However, they believed that the resulting campaign and "frenzy" of public accusations against individual men was unjustified and disempowered women while serving the interests of the "enemies of sexual freedom, the religious extremists, the reactionaries."

It is a fundamental principle of most democratic legal systems that a person is innocent until proven guilty. In this respect, the French authors are correct. Indeed, Article 11 of the *Universal Declaration of Human Rights* – the foundation of the international human rights law system – states:

Everyone charged with a penal offence has the right to be presumed innocent until proved guilty according to law in a public trial at which he has had all the guarantees necessary for his defence.[20]

Nevertheless, the French authors seem to minimise many forms of "less serious" harassment, such as "a man who rubs himself against her in the subway" or who raises intimate topics of conversation at a work function, or who sends a work colleague sexually charged messages. They claimed that, while this may be offensive to the woman concerned, it could be regarded "as the expression of a great sexual deprivation, or even as a non-event."[21]

Unfortunately, this misses the point of sexual harassment. Sexual harassment is generally understood as an unwelcome sexual advance, unwelcome request for sexual favours or other unwelcome conduct of a sexual nature which makes a person feel offended, humiliated and/or intimidated, where a reasonable person would anticipate that reaction in the circumstances.[22] This combines a *subjective* element (the response of the person affected) and an *objective* element (the reasonableness of that response).

If the affected woman feels offended, humiliated, or intimidated in circumstances where a reasonable person would respond similarly, it *is* sexual harassment. If another woman reacts to the same situation differently – perhaps not taking offence, or even feeling flattered – that is her prerogative. Clearly, in the latter case, it would *not* be sexual harassment.

The diversity of women's (and men's) experiences of sexual harassment and assault must be acknowledged, recognising individuals' different perspectives and responses. It is unhelpful to label, as the French authors did, any woman as sexually repressive or a prude because she takes offence to the man who rubs his groin against her on the subway or shares inappropriate sexual exploits with colleagues in the workplace.

How should business address sexual harassment in the workplace?

Businesses must take all reasonable steps to prevent sexual harassment and discrimination occurring in their workplaces.

This includes designing appropriate policies and procedures that support a harassment-free environment for all employees. Once these policies are established, it is critical that they are implemented across the organisation, with the support of senior management, and that staff at all levels receive suitable (and ongoing) training in them. The business should undertake ongoing human rights due diligence to continuously monitor risks of harassment (and other human rights risks) and respond to them.

In addition, a business should also consider introducing effective complaints mechanisms to deal with allegations of harassment and discrimination when they occur. According to the UN Guiding Principles, it is essential that these mechanisms are: legitimate, accessible, predictable, equitable, transparent, rights-compatible, a source of continuous learning, and based on engagement and dialogue with the stakeholders for whose use they are intended.[23]

Part IV examines in more detail the actions a company should take to address the human rights-related risks in its business and supply chain.

Can a business be held liable for sexual harassment committed by an employee?

In short: yes. In many jurisdictions (including Australia, the United Kingdom,[24] and the United States), an employer or principal can be held vicariously liable for sexual harassment committed by its employees or agents in connection with their duties unless all reasonable steps were taken by the employer to prevent sexual harassment occurring. Notably, the responsibility to demonstrate that all reasonable steps were taken rests with the employer.[25]

Where to from here?

This chapter started with an overview of the MeToo Movement and the allegations against Hollywood producer Harvey Weinstein. If these complaints lie at the most severe end of the continuum, it must also be acknowledged that there are many, many other instances of "garden variety" sexual harassment that occur every day in workplaces around the world and that often go uncommented upon. Accordingly, I close the chapter with an example of one of these situations.

The example comes from my own experience and occurred several years ago during a business meeting. The casual and incidental nature of the interaction contributes to its insidiousness. After the encounter, I posted the account below on the online business networking platform LinkedIn, partly seeking to make sense of the interaction to myself, but also hoping (in some very small way) to raise awareness of these issues more broadly. After posting, I was disappointed but not surprised to receive responses from many colleagues and friends (mainly women, but also men) who have also experienced sexual harassment in the workplace. This has underscored for me the crucial importance of maintaining vigilance on this issue in our workplaces: raising awareness to prevent sexual harassment in the first place, and providing access to complaint handling mechanisms and remedy when it does occur.

Calling out "casual" sexual harassment in the workplace

In a recent business meeting, I found myself speechless.

You see, the conversation had taken an abrupt turn. From discussing various developments in international and domestic politics – the main topic of our meeting – the businessman with whom I was speaking referred obliquely to his employer, a major television network:

"If we were having an affair, they would know which hotel we were staying in every night."

My stomach turned. My mind catapulted from an interesting, professional conversation to a hotel room. This man. Twice my age. With his pants down. I had to supress my instinct to run or vomit.

He went on: "Do you mind if I ask your age?"

I did mind, but told him anyway; despite the fact that it seemed completely irrelevant to our discussion.

"That's amazing! You look incredible for such an old girl. The women back at the office would be so envious of your skin!"

Dumbfounded, I should have stopped him there. But while I was still collecting my dignity from the floor, he continued to blunder on....

"Do you have any children?"

I told him no, and he helpfully suggested that I had better get a move along. "Women are leaving it far too late these days." He offered his opinions freely and unselfconsciously, completely oblivious to the impact it was having on me.

Appalled and embarrassed, I steered the conversation back to matters of business: the purpose of our meeting to begin with.

Not long after this, the meeting ended and we went our separate ways.

Afterwards – as so often happens – I thought of a million witty ripostes and comebacks. I was kicking myself for being rendered mute and for not asserting myself better in the moment.

Sexual harassment comes in many different forms – both explicit and implicit. Its impact can be insidious and unexpected, silencing even those of us – like me – who would usually be outspoken on these issues.

Reflecting on it later, I realise now that my reaction was a common one: I tried to ignore his offensive comments and deflect back to the topic of our meeting. In my mind, I minimised their seriousness – partly not to appear shrill or overreactive, and partly not to burn a bridge with an influential contact.

Shock definitely has a role to play too. This was the last thing I expected to encounter from a prominent and influential businessman at 10am in the morning over a cup of tea!

It's incredible, but not surprising, that this kind of behaviour continues in workplaces around the world in the twenty-first century. It doesn't seem to matter who you are or what you do. Whether you're the Prime Minister, a surgeon or a human rights lawyer – anyone can be affected.

Together, we all need to call sexual harassment out – whatever form it comes in, and wherever it occurs.

Notes

1 UN General Assembly, *Convention on the Elimination of All Forms of Discrimination against Women*, 18 December 1979, United Nations, Treaty Series, vol. 1249, p. 13. Accessed on 15 September 2018: www.refworld.org/docid/3ae6b3970.html.

2 UN General Assembly, *Declaration on the Elimination of Violence against Women*, 20 December 1993, A/RES/48/104. Accessed on 15 September 2018: www.refworld.org/docid/3b00f25d2c.html.

3 International Labour Organization (ILO), *Discrimination (Employment and Occupation) Convention, C111*, 25 June 1958, C111. Accessed on 15 September 2018: www.refworld.org/docid/3ddb 680f4.html.

4 Kantor, Jodi and Twohey, Megan. "Harvey Weinstein paid off sexual harassment accusers for decades." *New York Times*, 5 October 2017. Accessed on 2 June 2018: www.nytimes.com/2017/10/05/us/harvey-weinstein-harassment-allegations.html.

5 Farrow, Ronan. "Sexual assault: Harvey Weinstein's accusers tell their stories." *The New Yorker*, 10 October 2017. Accessed on 2 June 2018: www.newyorker.com/news/news-desk/from-aggressive-overtures-to-sexual-assault-harvey-weinsteins-accusers-tell-their-stories.

6 Gabler, Ellen, Twohey, Megan, and Kantor, Jodi. "New accusers expand Harvey Weinstein sexual assault claims back to the 70s." *New York Times*, 30 October 2017. Accessed on 3 June 2018: www.nytimes.com/2017/10/30/us/harvey-weinstein-sexual-assault-allegations.html.

7 Andreeva, Nellie. "Seth MacFarlane opens up about his 2013 Harvey Weinstein Oscars joke, condemns "abhorrent" abuse of power," 11 October 2017. Accessed on 3 June 2018: https://deadline.com/2017/10/seth-macfarlane-harvey-weinstein-oscar-joke-explained-1202186425.

8 *Chen-Oster* v. *Goldman Sachs, Inc.*, Case No. 10–6950 (S.D.N.Y.).

9 Goldman Gender Case. Accessed on 4 June 2018: http://goldman gendercase.com.

10 *H. Cristina Chen-Oster, Lisa Parisi, Shanna Orlich, Allison Gamba, and Mary De Luis* v. *Goldman, Sachs & Co and The Goldman Sachs Group Inc.*, S.D.N.Y., filed: 3/30/2018. Accessed on 27 July 2018: http://goldmangendercase.com/wp-content/uploads/2018/03/Dkt_578-OPINION-AND-ORDER.pdf.

11 Mayer, Jane and Farrow, Ronan. "Four women accuse New York's attorney general of physical abuse." *The New Yorker*, 7 May 2018.

12 As above.

13 Stempel, Jonathan. "21st Century Fox in $90 million settlement tied to sexual harassment scandal." Reuters, 20 November 2017.

Accessed on 3 June 2018: www.reuters.com/article/us-fox-settlement/ 21st-century-fox-in-90-million-settlement-tied-to-sexual-harassment- scandal-idUSKBN1DK2NI.

14 MEAA. "Employer investigations, employee rights and sexual har- assment at work," 26 September 2017. Accessed on 4 June 2018: www.meaa.org/news/employer-investigations-employee-rights-and- sexual-harassment-at-work.

15 *Moussouris* v. *Microsoft Corporation*, Case No. C15–1483JLR.

16 Microsoft Gender Case. Accessed on 4 June 2018: https://microsoft gendercase.com.

17 As above.

18 "Full translation of French anti-#Me-Too manifesto signed by Catherine Deneuve." World Crunch, 1 January 2018. Accessed on 5 June 2018: www.worldcrunch.com/opinion-analysis/full-translation- of-french-anti-metoo-manifesto-signed-by-catherine-deneuve.

19 As above.

20 Article 11, UN General Assembly (1948), *Universal Declaration of Human Rights* (217 [III] A). Paris.

21 As above, note 106.

22 Legal definition of sexual harassment, Australian Human Rights Commission. Accessed on 5 June 2018: www.humanrights.gov. au/publications/sexual-harassment-workplace-legal-definition-sexual- harassment.

23 Principle 31 (Effectiveness criteria for non-judicial grievance mecha- nisms), UN Guiding Principles.

24 Following the decision in *Lister* v. *Hesley Hall Ltd* ([2012] 1 AC 215), vicarious liability in the UK has been expanded to better cover intentional torts, such as sexual assault and deceit.

25 Australian Human Rights Commission, Chapter 3.1, Sexual Harass- ment (A Code in Practice) – Liability. Accessed on 5 June 2018: www.humanrights.gov.au/publications/sexual-harassment-code- practice-liability.

Part IV

Getting started – what actions should a company take?

It is understandable that some corporate executives may feel perplexed and even, at times, overwhelmed by the plethora of legal and non-legal obligations they face relating to human rights. A multinational corporation operating across various legal jurisdictions will be subject to an array of legislation touching on human rights (and related issues) impacting their business. Likewise, as outlined in Chapter 7, there are many multi-stakeholder initiatives – both general and industry-specific – that a company may be called on to join and implement. It is rarely possible to join everything. And, even if it was, it is questionable whether this would be desirable anyway.

This leads us to an important question: what does the corporate responsibility to respect human rights under the UN Guiding Principles mean in *practical* terms? What actions should a company take to get started? Part IV addresses these questions directly. While each company's situation and experiences will inevitably be unique and there is no one-size-fits-all approach, the following chapters seek to provide some general guidance (drawn from the UN Guiding Principles) that will benefit all businesses.

Chapter 10

Developing a human rights policy

Policies and procedures are crucial mechanisms governing most organisations, whether they are in government or the private sector. Policies provide an important road map or blueprint to guide decision-making and behaviour. They also assist organisations to achieve clarity and consistency throughout their operations, and to communicate this information both internally and externally to their stakeholders.

In the context of business's responsibility to respect human rights, developing a human rights policy or statement is particularly important. Companies can cause, or contribute to, adverse impacts on human rights through their own activities, and through their business relationships. Given this, the process of systematically considering all the facets of a company's operations and its impacts on human rights can be very illuminating. In many instances, in the process of developing their human rights policy, companies have uncovered various issues that were previously overlooked. On the other hand, without a human rights policy, a company seeking to respect human rights is fumbling along in the darkness without a torch.

While many existing company policies may touch on human rights-related issues, they are usually not framed explicitly in human rights terms. Also, such policies often consider the issues from the perspective of risks to the company – rather than risks to rights-holders (who may be external to the company). Some examples include: occupational health and safety, bullying and harassment, and diversity policies.

Human rights policy: UNGP 16

UN Guiding Principle 16 provides guidance on how to develop a human rights policy. The policy should set out the company's approach to identifying, preventing, mitigating, and accounting for its adverse human rights impacts.

It should also include an explicit commitment by the company to respect *all* internationally recognised human rights standards. This includes, at a minimum, the International Bill of Rights (comprising the *Universal Declaration of Human Rights* and the main instruments through which it has been codified: the *International Covenant on Civil and Political Rights* and the *International Covenant on Economic, Social and Cultural Rights*), and the ILO's *Declaration on the Fundamental Principles and Rights at Work*.[1]

UN Guiding Principle 16 states:

> As the basis for embedding their responsibility to respect human rights, business enterprises should express their commitment to meet this responsibility through a statement of policy that:
>
> (a) Is approved at the most senior level of the business enterprise;
>
> (b) Is informed by relevant internal and/or external expertise;
>
> (c) Stipulates the enterprise's human rights expectations of personnel, business partners and other parties directly linked to its operations, products or services;
>
> (d) Is publicly available and communicated internally and externally to all personnel, business partners and other relevant parties;
>
> (e) Is reflected in operational policies and procedures necessary to embed it throughout the business enterprise.[2]

The Commentary to UN Guiding Principle 16 underscores how important it is for business to ensure coherence between its responsibility to respect human rights and the policies and procedures that govern its wider business activities and relationships.

Like States, it is possible that some policies governing wider areas of a business's activities may stand in tension to its human rights policy. The Commentary cites a couple of examples: policies and procedures that set financial and other performance incentives for personnel; procurement practices; and lobbying activities where human rights are at stake. The key challenge is to achieve consistency throughout *all* policies.

Where should a company begin?

In developing a human rights policy, a good strategy is to consider the particular kinds of human rights issues and risks facing a business, and its industry more broadly. By contextualising the issues in this way, the resulting human rights policy is likely to be more relevant and targeted to the specific needs of a business. For example, for a social media or internet company, the rights to privacy and to freedom of expression are likely to be paramount; for a confectionary company sourcing cocoa from developing countries, labour rights and working conditions are likely to be key considerations.

The Office of the UN High Commissioner for Human Rights and the UN Global Compact has developed a useful guide, *How to Develop a Human Rights Policy* ("the Guide").[3] Some key steps it recommends are to:

- assign senior management responsibility to drive the process;
- involve cross-functional personnel (human resources, legal, procurement, security) in the process to build understanding, know-how, and a sense of common purpose;
- identify and draw on internal and/or external human rights expertise;
- map existing company policies to identify human rights coverage and gaps;

- conduct a basic mapping of the company's key potential human rights impacts;
- consult internal and external stakeholders to identify and respond to their expectations;
- communicate the policy internally and externally; and
- reflect human rights policy in operational policies and procedures.[4]

What form should a human rights policy or statement take?

The UN Guiding Principles are not prescriptive about the form a human rights policy or statement should take. Recognising that companies have different capacities and processes based on various factors (including their size, sector, and structure, and the severity of the human rights risks they face), they acknowledge that "respective policies and processes will take on different forms."[5]

Generally, companies choose one of two approaches: either a stand-alone policy on human rights or an integrated approach, weaving human rights into their other policies and codes of conduct. In 2009, John Ruggie reflected that there are advantages and disadvantages to both options. He said:

> An advantage cited for free-standing procedures is that the relevant issues get the attention and professionalization they deserve. But a disadvantage may be that it is not connected to the rest of the company. In contrast, folding human rights due diligence into ongoing processes may put human rights on par with other key issues when managers evaluate potential projects, but the unique attributes of human rights may thereby get diminished.[6]

Ultimately, this matter will be determined by the circumstances of each company and the context in which it operates. The Guide states that "Stand-alone or free-standing policies have an advantage in external communication, making it easier for interested stakeholders to access information they require."[7]

However, on the other hand, for companies with well-established codes of conduct, the Guide considers that an integrated approach may be preferable as it avoids having multiple standards in place. In addition, it acknowledges that "Integrated policies can suggest that human rights considerations are more deeply engrained within the company's overall thinking, which can appeal to external stakeholders."[8]

Notes

1 UN Guiding Principle 12 affirms that this is the scope (at a minimum) of business's responsibility to respect internationally recognised human rights.
2 *UN Guiding Principles on Business and Human Rights*, Principle 16, p. 16.
3 UN High Commissioner for Human Rights and the UN Global Compact, *How to Develop a Human Rights Policy*, 2nd ed., 2015. Accessed on 22 June 2018: www.unglobalcompact.org/library/22.
4 As above, p. 2.
5 Commentary to UN Guiding Principle 14.
6 A/HRC/11/13.
7 UN High Commissioner for Human Rights and the UN Global Compact, *How to Develop a Human Rights Policy*, 2nd ed., 2015. Accessed on 22 June 2018: www.unglobalcompact.org/library/22.
8 As above.

Chapter 11

Assessing the risks of human rights violations in the supply chain

Assessing the risks of human rights violations in a company's supply chain is essential for determining where the greatest risks lie and how they might be addressed. As part of this, companies should consider conducting a human rights impact assessment ("HRIA"), examining the business's direct operations, its supply chain, and other business relationships.

In simple terms, an HRIA is a process for identifying, understanding, assessing, and addressing the adverse effects of a business's activities on the human rights of workers, communities, consumers, or other rights-holders.[1]

Identifying and assessing human rights impacts: UNGP 18

Under the UN Guiding Principles, identifying and assessing the human rights impacts of a company is the first step in the process of conducting human rights due diligence (the topic of human rights due diligence will be discussed in more detail in Chapter 12).

UN Guiding Principle 18 states (in part):

> In order to gauge human rights risks, business enterprises should identify and assess any actual or potential adverse human rights impacts with which they may be involved either through their own activities or as a result of their business relationships.[2]

This means understanding the specific impacts of a business in a particular set of circumstances. As the Commentary to UN Guiding Principle 18 clarifies,

> Typically this includes assessing the human rights context prior to a proposed business activity, where possible; identifying who may be affected; cataloguing the relevant human rights standards and issues; and projecting how the proposed activity and associated business relationships could have adverse human rights impacts on those identified.[3]

Given that human rights situations are dynamic and constantly changing, it is essential that impact assessments occur regularly at key points throughout a project or business relationship, for example before commencing a new project or business relationship, before major decisions or changes are made, or in response to problems in the business's operating environment.

As part of this process, the UN Guiding Principles underscore the importance of drawing on internal and/or independent external human rights expertise and consulting affected stakeholders in a meaningful way to ensure their views are properly taken into consideration.

Prioritising the most severe human rights risks: UNGP 24

Once human rights risks have been identified, a critical question is: how should they be prioritised?

The UN Guiding Principles state that business should address *all* their adverse impacts on human rights. However, in practice, given the scope and range of many businesses' activities it is often not possible to address all human rights impacts simultaneously. Where this is the case, UN Guiding Principle 24 states that:

> business enterprises should first seek to prevent and mitigate those that are most severe or where delayed response would make them irremediable.[4]

The table below illustrates how human rights risks might be prioritised effectively by considering the factors of scale, scope, and remediability. It emphasises that prioritisation is a relative exercise. Each of the relevant factors in the circumstances must be taken into consideration to determine what constitutes the greatest risks for human rights.

Table 11.1 Factors for prioritising human rights risks

Factors	Definition	Examples
Scale	The gravity or seriousness of the adverse impact on human rights.	• Interference with fundamental rights and freedoms like access to a living wage, freedom of expression, or the right to life.
Scope	The extent or reach of the impact. For example, how many people would be affected?	• A couple of individuals • A whole community
Remediability	Whether it would be possible to restore affected individuals to their previous situation (or an equivalent situation), after the harm occurs.	• A local worker is underpaid and so is unable to afford the basic necessities of life, such as food, housing, and water. The worker's pay can be reviewed and increased to an appropriate level, with an apology provided and compensation paid to rectify the underpayment. • A worker is killed on site due to a lack of health and safety measures.

Features indicating heightened risk

Given the extent of many corporations' supply chains, it is difficult for many organisations to know where to start when assessing their potential human rights risks and impacts.

In 2016, CORE, a UK civil society coalition on corporate accountability, produced a guide outlining several features that could indicate a heightened risk of human rights violations in a supply chain.[5] Specifically, a company's business model, "operating context," and the nature and location of its work should be taken into consideration when assessing risks in the supply chain.

Each of these elements are briefly outlined below and are a useful starting point for companies seeking to understand their potential human rights risks.

I Business models

- Subcontracting and complex supply chains: as supply chains extend and business relationships become more complex, monitoring and management becomes more difficult. As a result, the risk of human rights violations in the supply chain increases.
- Extended or complex employment relationships: the risk of exploitation of workers through unscrupulous or illegal practices increases in sectors employing high numbers of agency, outsourced, or subcontracted workers. As the relationship between worker and employer becomes less direct and transparent, the employer may not be aware of the conditions workers are being subjected to. Likewise, the presence of labour brokers or recruiters in the supply chain can heighten risks of human rights violations. Some unscrupulous practices include contract substitution and the imposition of debt or recruitment fees on workers.
- High flexibility and low-profit margins: rapid production timeframes and the demand for high flexibility needed to adjust to quickly changing requirements can increase

workers' vulnerability to exploitation. This can especially occur in consumer-driven sectors and includes unreasonably long working hours, forced overtime (often without adequate pay), and unsafe work conditions.

2 Operating context

- The risk of human rights violations increases in countries lacking laws or regulations protecting human rights and labour standards. Further, where laws do exist, the agencies responsible for enforcing them may lack the power or resources to do so.
- The presence of cheap labour and high numbers of vulnerable workers: some workers are likely to be more vulnerable to exploitation than others. These include women, children, migrants, minorities, and workers with a disability.
- The absence of effective and representative workers' organisations or collective agreements: the risk of human rights abuses is heightened where workers are discouraged or prevented from joining a union, or where collective agreements do not represent workers' perspectives.

3 Nature and location of the work

- Work that relies on low-skilled or unskilled labour is often low paid and may employ workers who are vulnerable or marginalised. Such workers may also be less aware of their rights than better educated workers.
- Work of a dangerous or physically demanding nature places workers at greater risk, particularly where protections for workers' health and safety are inadequate.
- Home-based workers and workers employed in informal enterprises generally operate in unmonitored and unregulated environments, where they are at increased risk of abuse.

Notes

1 See: Business and Human Rights Resource Centre website. Accessed on 21 June 2018: www.business-humanrights.org/en/un-guiding-principles/implementation-tools-examples/implementation-by-companies/type-of-step-taken/human-rights-impact-assessments.
2 *UN Guiding Principles on Business and Human Rights*, Principle 18, p. 19.
3 Commentary to *UN Guiding Principles on Business and Human Rights*, Principle 18, p. 19.
4 *UN Guiding Principles on Business and Human Rights*, Principle 24, p. 26.
5 CORE Coalition, *Beyond Compliance: Effective Reporting Under the Modern Slavery Act: A Civil Society Guide for Commercial Organisations on the Transparency in Supply Chains Clause*, 2016, p. 9. Accessed on 21 June 2018: http://corporate-responsibility.org/wp-content/uploads/2016/03/CSO_TISC_guidance_final_digitalversion_16.03.16.pdf.

Chapter 12

Human rights due diligence

Like developing a human rights policy, conducting human rights due diligence is also essential for all businesses seeking to meet their responsibility to respect under the UN Guiding Principles.

From the outset, it should be noted that human rights due diligence is different from standard corporate due diligence. While corporate due diligence assesses the risks to a company *itself*, human rights due diligence means examining the human rights risks not only to the company, but also to individuals and community groups adversely impacted by it. In this way, it represents a paradigm shift.

Another crucial difference between standard corporate due diligence and human rights due diligence is that the latter is ongoing, continuous and iterative reflecting the complex and changing nature of human rights risks. While corporate due diligence is often undertaken at a key juncture in a project or transaction, for example prior to the acquisition of an asset by a company or before investing in a project, human rights due diligence should be regular and can occur simultaneously with other steps – such as updating and implementing corporate policies that respect human rights.

What does human rights due diligence mean?

UN Guiding Principle 17 clarifies the meaning of human rights due diligence. It states:

In order to identify, prevent, mitigate and account for how they address their adverse human rights impacts, business enterprises should carry out human rights due diligence. The process should include assessing *actual and potential* human rights impacts, integrating and acting upon the findings, tracking responses, and communicating how impacts are addressed. Human rights due diligence:

(a) Should cover adverse human rights impacts that the business enterprise *may cause or contribute to* through its *own activities*, or which may be *directly linked* to its operations, products or services by its *business relationships*;

(b) Will vary in complexity with the size of the business enterprise, the risk of severe human rights impacts, and the nature and context of its operations;

(c) Should be ongoing, recognizing that the human rights risks may change over time as the business enterprise's operations and operating context evolve [emphases added].

In other words, according to UN Guiding Principle 17, there are three ways business can be involved in human rights harm. Each of these should be assessed as part of the human rights diligence process:

• Where a business enterprise causes, or may cause, an adverse human rights impact through its own activities.

• Where a business enterprise contributes, or may contribute, to an adverse human rights impact through its own activities.

• Where a business enterprise has not contributed to an adverse human rights impact, but that impact is nevertheless directly linked to its operations, products or services by its business relationship with another entity.

How far should companies go in carrying out human rights due diligence?

• Prioritise areas where the risk of human rights impacts is most significant

For multinational companies with a large number of subsidiaries and other entities in their corporate structure, carrying out human rights due diligence across the entire company may be extremely difficult. The UN Guiding Principles recognise this and state that, if this is the case:

> [b]usiness enterprises should identify general areas where the risk of adverse human rights impacts is most significant, whether due to certain suppliers' or clients' operating context, the particular operations, products or services involved, or other relevant considerations, and prioritize these for human rights due diligence.[1]

• Impacts directly linked to its business relationships

In addition to the human rights impacts that a business causes or contributes to through its *own activities*, human rights due diligence should also cover adverse impacts which may be directly linked to its operations, products or services *by its business relationships*.

Professor Ruggie has clarified that there are two ways that businesses can be involved in adverse impacts on human rights through their business relationships:

1   where the enterprise contributes to harm caused by a third party, and
2   where the enterprise neither causes nor contributes but its operations, products or services are directly linked through its business relationships to the harm.[2]

Likewise, the guide *Frequently Asked Questions about the Guiding Principles on Business and Human Rights* ("FAQ

Guide") clarifies the meaning of "business relationships." These are defined broadly as: "relationships with business partners, entities in its value chain and any other State or non-State entity directly linked to its business operations, products or services."[3] Notably (and somewhat counterintuitively given the reference to "directly linked" in UN Guiding Principle 17(a)), the FAQ Guide states that this also incorporates *indirect* business relationships and entities beyond the first tier in a company's supply chain.

The UN Guiding Principles acknowledge the added complexity involved when a business has not contributed to an adverse human rights impact, but that impact is nevertheless directly linked to a company by its business relationships. It states:

> Among the factors that will enter into the determination of the appropriate action in such situations are the enterprise's leverage over the entity concerned, how crucial the relationship is to the enterprise, the severity of the abuse, and whether terminating the relationship with the entity itself would have adverse human rights consequences.[4]

When conducting human rights due diligence beyond the first tier in the supply chain, it may be helpful for companies to engage in "collective action" with other partners, for example with local civil society groups, academic and human rights experts, and operational-level and State-based grievance mechanisms.

However, there are many circumstances in which the most appropriate response may be for the company to end its relationship with the entity adversely impacting human rights. This might include: where the company lacks leverage over the entity and is unable to increase it, and/or where the human rights impacts are severe in nature.

While the abuse is ongoing, a company will need to accept any potential consequences of its continuing relationship with the entity. Financial and reputational consequences are two aspects for a company to consider. Even more significant in most cases, though, are the possible legal consequences.

• *Complicity: indirect involvement by companies in human rights abuses*

In considering the scope of their human rights due diligence programmes, companies should also be mindful of the concept of complicity. For some time, corporate complicity has been a somewhat amorphous concept in legal jurisprudence under which companies may be liable under criminal or civil law for their involvement in wrongs.

In his 2008 report, Professor Ruggie stated that "the corporate responsibility to respect human rights includes avoiding complicity." He clarified, stating that this:

> refers to indirect involvement by companies in human rights abuses – where the actual harm is committed by another party, including governments and non-State actors. Due diligence can help a company avoid complicity.[5]

Under international criminal law, aiding and abetting (or complicity) is defined as "knowingly providing practical assistance or encouragement that has a substantial effect on the commission of a crime."[6] Likewise, under the law of numerous national jurisdictions, corporations can be held criminally liable for complicity.

In practical terms, it is sometimes difficult to discern whether a company's actions or omissions will be considered complicit. Professor Ruggie has clarified that merely being present in a country and paying taxes is unlikely to create liability, but deriving indirect economic benefit from the wrongful conduct of others may be enough to do so, depending on the specific facts in each case.[7] What is clear, though, is that:

> even where a corporation does not intend for the crime to occur, and regrets its commission, it will not be absolved of liability if it knew, or should have known, that it was providing assistance, and that the assistance would contribute to the commission of a crime.[8]

In any case, if a corporation has concerns that it could be complicit in human rights abuses of any kind, it should obtain expert legal advice immediately.

Do all companies have the same obligations in relation to human rights due diligence?

The responsibility to respect human rights is a baseline expectation that applies to *all* companies, irrespective of their size, structure, operating context, sector, or industry. Having said this, factors such as a company's size, structure, and sector may influence the *approach* it adopts to meeting its responsibility to respect human rights.

As UN Guiding Principle 17(b) clarifies, human rights due diligence "will vary in complexity with the size of the business enterprise, the risk of severe human rights impacts, and the nature and context of its operations." For example, a larger company with a complex, multinational supply chain that encompasses many business relationships and employees will, in most cases, need to have more formal and comprehensive systems in place to ensure it satisfies its responsibility to respect human rights.[9]

On the other hand, for a smaller company with fewer employees and a less complex supply chain, internal systems and processes for meeting the responsibility to respect may be less formal and diffuse. However, this is not always the case. The approach a company takes to human rights due diligence should always be guided first and foremost by the risk that the company's operations, products, services, and business relationships pose to human rights. Where the risks are high, the policies and processes adopted to human rights due diligence must reflect this.[10]

What if human rights abuses are discovered in the due diligence process? Won't this create legal liability for a company?

By conducting human rights due diligence, companies place themselves in the best position to identify, prevent, and respond to potential and actual human rights abuses as soon as possible. Should a legal claim subsequently arise against them, they can demonstrate that they took every reasonable step to avoid involvement with the alleged abuse.[11]

In their article "Human Rights Due Diligence: Is It Too Risky?" lawyers Amy Lehr and John Sherman examine this question from various perspectives.[12] In the course of the due diligence process, a company may uncover unwelcome facts of which it was previously unaware, requiring it to take action to prevent, mitigate, or remedy the abuses. Despite this, the authors conclude that "not conducting due diligence is too risky, for both business and society."[13] As acceptance grows of the UN Guiding Principles as the global standard of conduct expected of companies, this is likely to be even more the case.

Nonetheless, the UN Guiding Principles make it clear that human rights due diligence may *not* necessarily be sufficient to avoid liability. They state: "business enterprises conducting such due diligence should not assume that, by itself, this will automatically and fully absolve them from liability for causing or contributing to human rights abuses."[14]

Tracking responses

Tracking their responses to human rights abuses allows companies to verify whether their actions have been effective. According to UN Guiding Principle 20, tracking should incorporate qualitative and quantitative indicators and draw on feedback from internal and external sources, including affected stakeholders.

Tracking should be incorporated within a company's internal reporting processes, for example performance contracts and reviews, surveys, and audits.[15]

Communicating how impacts are addressed

Lastly, the Guiding Principles underscore the importance of companies communicating how human rights impacts are addressed. This provides a level of transparency and accountability for all stakeholders, and particularly for those whose human rights may have been impacted by a company.

UN Guiding Principle 21 states that communications should be accessible to their intended audiences, provide sufficient information to evaluate the adequacy of an enterprise's response to the human rights impact involved, and not pose risks to affected stakeholders or unduly compromise commercial confidentiality.[16]

Communications come in various forms. They may be more formal, such as annual reports, dedicated human rights, or corporate responsibility reports, or less formal, such as online updates and social media announcements. Likewise, they can include in-person meetings and stakeholder consultations.[17]

Additional guidance on due diligence

The OECD's *Due Diligence Guidance for Responsible Business Conduct* ("the Guidance") provides a very useful resource for companies seeking to conduct effective human rights due diligence.[18] The publication provides guidance on due diligence beyond just human rights. In addition, it covers due diligence in the areas of employment and industrial relations, the environment, combatting bribery, and consumer interests (among others). The Guidance is based on the *OECD Guidelines for Multinational Enterprises*, one of the multi-stakeholder initiatives mentioned in Chapter 7. As noted above, the OECD Guidelines were revised and updated after the UN Guiding Principles were released to incorporate them. As such, the documents are consistent.

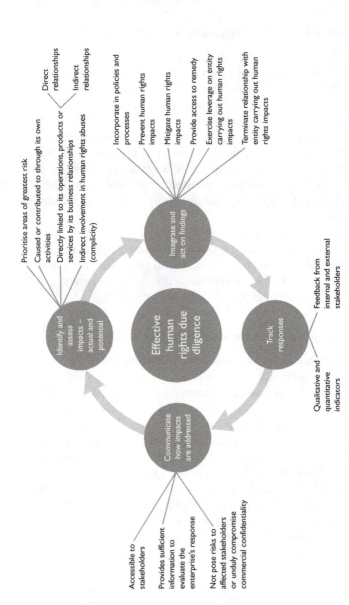

Figure 12.1 Effective human rights due diligence.

Note
Human rights due diligence must be ongoing, recognising the complex and constantly changing nature of companies' supply chains and business relationships. This figure summarises the process.

Notes

1 Commentary to UN Guiding Principle 17, p. 18.
2 Ruggie, John G. "Comments on Thun Group of Banks discussion paper on the implications of UN Guiding Principles 13 & 17 in a corporate and investment banking context," 21 February 2017, p. 1. Accessed on 10 July 2018: www.business-humanrights.org/sites/default/files/documents/Thun%20Final.pdf.
3 *Frequently Asked Questions about the Guiding Principles on Business and Human Rights*, Question 33, p. 32. Accessed on 1 July 2018: www.ohchr.org/documents/publications/faq_principlesbussiness hr.pdf.
4 Commentary to UN Guiding Principle 19, pp. 21–22.
5 *Protect, Respect, and Remedy: A Framework for Business and Human Rights*, A/HRC/8/5, April 2008, p. 20.
6 Commentary to UN Guiding Principle 17, p. 19.
7 A/HRC/4/035, p. 11, para 32.
8 As above.
9 *Frequently Asked Questions about the Guiding Principles on Business and Human Rights*, Question 33, p. 32. Accessed on 1 July 2018: www.ohchr.org/documents/publications/faq_principlesbussiness hr.pdf.
10 As above.
11 Commentary to UN Guiding Principle 17, p. 19.
12 Sherman, John and Lehr, Amy. 2010. "Human rights due diligence: Is it too risky?" Corporate Social Responsibility Initiative Working Paper No. 55, John F. Kennedy School of Government, Harvard University, 2010.
13 As above, p. 22.
14 Commentary to UN Guiding Principle 17, p. 19.
15 Commentary to UN Guiding Principle 20, p. 23.
16 UN Guiding Principle 21, p. 23.
17 Commentary to UN Guiding Principle 21, p. 24.
18 OECD (2018), *OECD Due Diligence Guidance for Responsible Business Conduct*. Accessed on 29 July 2018: www.oecd.org/investment/due-diligence-guidance-for-responsible-business-conduct.htm.

Chapter 13

Access to remedy and grievance mechanisms

The need for victims of corporate human rights abuses to have access to effective remedy is the third arm of Professor Ruggie's UN Framework (outlined in Chapter 1), and so comprises a critical part of the UN Guiding Principles.

When should a corporation provide remediation for its involvement in human rights impacts?

UN Guiding Principle 22 provides:

> Where business enterprises identify that they have caused or contributed to adverse impacts, they should provide for or cooperate in their remediation through legitimate processes.[1]

The Commentary to Guiding Principle 22 elaborates that one way a business might provide remediation is through an operational-level grievance mechanism (as discussed further below). In other cases, remediation may be provided by another entity. For example, if criminal charges are involved, the company should defer to and cooperate with the legal proceedings.

However, the Commentary also clarifies that, when adverse impacts occur that:

> the business enterprise has not caused or contributed to, but which are *directly linked* to its operations, products or

services by a business relationship, the responsibility to respect human rights does *not require* that the enterprise itself provide for remediation, though it may take a role in doing so [emphasis added].[2]

Guiding Principle 22 seems to provide a relatively clear delineation between when a corporation *should* provide remediation for its involvement in adverse impacts on human rights and when it *may* choose to do so. Nevertheless, companies would be well advised not to adopt an unduly restrictive approach to interpreting their responsibilities to provide remediation for the human rights impacts with which they are involved.

There are two reasons for this. First, different perspectives may be taken on a company's involvement in the human rights abuses at issue: that is, whether a company causes or contributes to adverse impacts on human rights, or is "merely" linked to them, might be a contested matter and cannot necessarily be accurately determined by a company in advance.[3] Second, as a matter of public perception, a company that is directly linked to adverse impacts on human rights through a business relationship, inevitably, cannot escape disapprobation for them.

Chapter 17 below outlines a case study from the banking and finance sector relevant to these issues. By adopting a minimalist and limited interpretation of banks' responsibilities for human rights impacts with which they were involved, the Thun Group of Banks' 2017 discussion paper generated vehement criticism and opposition from the business and human rights global community. To a large extent, the Thun Group's paper detracts from and undermines much of the progress already achieved by the banking sector on these issues. This experience should act as a cautionary tale for other corporations (and industry groups) seeking to take a narrow approach to interpreting their responsibilities to respect human rights.

State-based and non-State-based remedies

Remedy processes (or grievance mechanisms) come in a range of forms and can provide a variety of potential outcomes for victims. These include: financial or non-financial compensation, apologies, restitution, rehabilitation, punitive sanctions, and mechanisms for the prevention of harm.[4]

State-based grievance mechanisms include judicial and non-judicial processes and may be administered by an agency of the State or by an independent statutory body.

Judicial processes can include claims in civil or criminal proceedings against the corporation alleged to have committed, or contributed to, the human rights abuse. While sometimes the best option, it must be noted that judicial proceedings are invariably extremely costly and time-consuming for all parties involved. These factors must be taken into consideration by victims seeking remedy for human rights harms, and may determine the course they choose to take.

Non-judicial State-based grievance mechanisms vary from State to State but might include, for example, State-appointed ombudspersons, complaints handling mechanisms under a country's national human rights institution, national contact points under the OECD Guidelines for Multinational Enterprises, or through other government-run complaints offices.

Non-State-based grievance mechanisms are also very important to consider in this context and include any procedure or process through which affected persons can bring their complaint against the company, have it heard, and have access to a process for settling their complaint.[5] The Commentary to Guiding Principle 28 clarifies that non-State-based grievance mechanisms encompass, among others, those administered by a business either alone or with stakeholders, by an industry association or a multi-stakeholder group.[6] This is often referred to as an "operational-level grievance mechanism."

What are the benefits of operational-level grievance mechanisms?

There are various benefits of using operational-level grievance mechanisms, for both companies and victims alleging corporate human rights abuses.

Practically, they have several advantages: the potential speed of these mechanisms (both in terms of accessing them and obtaining an outcome in a complaint), their reduced costs compared to litigation, and their transnational reach. From a company's perspective, these mechanisms enable grievances to be addressed early and directly by the business, thereby preventing grievances (and the harm resulting from them) from escalating.[7]

From an operational perspective, there are additional benefits. Through operational-level grievance mechanisms, companies obtain essential information on trends and patterns in complaints which can feed into their ongoing human rights due diligence process, enabling them to respond and adapt their business practices accordingly.[8]

Table 13.1 Overview of grievance mechanisms

Location (State or non-State)	Type
State-based grievance mechanisms	• Judicial • Non-judicial, e.g. ombudspersons; national human rights institutions' complaint processes; OECD national contact points.

Non-State-based grievance mechanisms	• Non-judicial
	  • Operational level (company)
	  • Regional and international human rights bodies

What makes a non-judicial grievance mechanism effective?

UN Guiding Principle 31 outlines the essential criteria for effective non-judicial grievance mechanisms (both State-based and non-State-based).[9] The criteria provide a "benchmark for designing, revising or assessing a non-judicial grievance mechanism to help ensure that it is effective in practice."[10] They are intended to be interdependent and mutually reinforcing. Accordingly, the criteria should be implemented as a whole.

In summary,[11] a grievance mechanism should be:

1   *Legitimate*: a grievance mechanism must be trusted by stakeholders and accountable for the fair conduct of its processes.
2   *Accessible*: stakeholders should be aware of the mechanism, and assistance should be provided to those facing certain barriers to access.
3   *Predictable*: the procedure should be clear and publicly communicated, including its indicative time frames for each stage and the types of outcome available.
4   *Equitable*: both parties should have reasonable access to information, advice and expert resources to engage in a process on fair, informed, and respectful terms.
5   *Transparent*: to support legitimacy and trust in the mechanism, parties should be regularly informed about a grievance's progress; and wider stakeholders should have sufficient information about the mechanism's performance to build confidence in its effectiveness.
6   *Rights-compatible*: ensuring that outcomes and remedies are consistent with internationally recognised human rights.
7   A *source of continuous learning*: regular analysis of grievances (their frequency, patterns, and causes) should be used to improve the mechanism itself, and to prevent future grievances and harms.

In addition to the seven criteria above, the UN Guiding Principles specify that an eighth criterion also applies to operational-level grievance mechanisms administered by business. To be effective, they should be:

8 *Based on engagement and dialogue*: to ensure a mechanism's legitimacy, its design and assessment of its performance should be based on consultations with affected stakeholders. If agreement cannot be reached between the business and stakeholders, an independent third party should adjudicate.

Notes

1 Guiding Principle 22, p. 24.
2 Commentary to Guiding Principle 22, pp. 24–25.
3 This point is affirmed by UN OHCHR's response (dated 12 June 2017) to a request from BankTrack for advice regarding the application of the UN Guiding Principles on Business and Human Rights in the context of the banking sector. In its advice, UN OHCHR states:

> it may be difficult in practice to delineate precisely whether a bank has contributed to an adverse impact or whether there is a situation of "direct linkage". However, since a bank's responsibility to respond to an impact (which may include remediation) depends on the nature of its involvement, it is nevertheless an important determination to make.
> (p. 5. Accessed on 12 July 2018: www.business-humanrights. org/sites/default/files/documents/Banktrack%20response_ FINAL.pdf)

4 Commentary to Guiding Principle 25, p. 27.
5 *Frequently Asked Questions about the Guiding Principles on Business and Human Rights*, Question 36 (What is a non-judicial grievance mechanism?), p. 36.
6 Commentary to Guiding Principle 28, p. 31.
7 Commentary to Guiding Principle 29, p. 32.
8 Commentary to Guiding Principle 29, p. 32.
9 Guiding Principle 31 and Commentary, pp. 33–35.
10 Commentary to Guiding Principle 31, p. 34.
11 This summary is drawn from UN Guiding Principle 31 and its Commentary.

Chapter 14

Locating business and human rights in an organisation

The preceding chapters have looked at some of the main substantive areas a company needs to consider to get started on its business and human rights journey. Having done this, we now arrive at an important question of form. That is, *where* is the best place to locate the business and human rights function within a corporation's organisational structure?

Previously, to the extent that corporations worked on human rights issues, they were often perceived as something falling into the category of *pro bono*, therefore voluntary work usually unrelated to core business. In some cases, this approach continues today. It is reflected, for example, in the practice of some global law firms which continue to locate their business and human rights function within their *pro bono* practice group.

In fact, as demonstrated in Chapter 6, business's responsibility to respect human rights is qualitatively different in nature from the general practice of *pro bono* law. Rather than considering a corporation's responsibility to respect human rights as volunteer work, or an optional *pro bono* activity if time permits, it must be recognised that human rights due diligence (and all that flows from it) is as critical and non-negotiable for business as corporate due diligence. That is, it must be a lens through which transactions and business relationships are continuously viewed to determine their probity.

Another common approach has been to locate human rights (or corporate social responsibility issues more broadly) within the marketing or public relations area of a corporation. This approach orientates human rights principally as a promotional opportunity for a corporation. While it is certainly true that positive marketing and public relations opportunities can arise as by-products of a corporation's work on human rights, making this the end goal itself misunderstands the very nature of business's responsibility to respect human rights. In addition, locating responsibility for these issues in the marketing area limits the efficacy of any human rights initiatives as they are functionally separate from the business's strategic operational areas.

A third approach has been to identify human rights and related concerns as predominantly a matter for the human resources area of a corporation. In some ways, this makes sense. The employees of a corporation are the principal beneficiaries of organisational initiatives designed to safeguard their workplace rights, conditions, and safety. Similarly, in many corporate disasters, employees have been among the groups most severely affected.

Nevertheless, the corporate responsibility to respect human rights is much broader than just respecting the rights of a corporation's employees. In fact, it extends much further to respect for the human rights of affected communities, and by contractors and suppliers involved in a corporation's work. As modern supply chains have become increasingly complicated and dispersed, a corporation has the potential to impact (directly and indirectly) a significant number of individuals connected with its operations.

Fortunately, as the business and human rights field has grown and matured, so too have corporations' approaches and organisational arrangements for managing these issues. Many corporations now treat human rights as an important legal and strategic issue for their business and, as such, integrate its management throughout the core functions of the organisation. One way this has been done successfully is to locate the business and human rights function within the legal and risk management area. This acknowledges the essential nature of human rights as a legal issue, and also enables a corporation to proactively monitor and address any emerging reputational risk issues arising from its impacts on human rights.

Lastly, for any corporation to successfully embed human rights throughout its organisation, it is absolutely essential that its senior leadership team and board both understand and support its importance. This is often much easier said than done. For many corporate executives coming fresh to business and human rights, it can sometimes seem tangential from their core business objectives and imperatives. As this book has sought to demonstrate, this is very far from the truth. Through greater education, training, and awareness, it is hoped that executives of all levels and in all functional areas can come to better understand the business of human rights.

Part V

Human rights snapshots from different sectors

To illustrate the crucial role that business can play in preventing and combatting human rights violations in its supply chain, Chapters 15 to 18 provide case studies from four different industries: apparel, fast-moving consumer goods, electronics, and banking and finance. While some of the issues and challenges described in these chapters may be unique to an industry, many will be shared by all industries. By examining four quite different industries, the ubiquity of human rights risks and challenges is highlighted.

Chapter 15

Apparel industry

Overview

Globally, the fashion industry is estimated to be worth US$1.2 trillion. It employs approximately 60 to 75 million people worldwide, around three-quarters of whom are female.[1]

"Fast fashion" is the movement to make fashion trends quickly and cheaply available to consumers. It moves at an unrelenting pace. Where once there were four seasonal fashion ranges produced per year, the major fashion retailers are now producing a dozen or more different ranges per year. Being mass-produced, the clothes are more affordable, thereby encouraging shoppers to buy more items and to shop more frequently. As you might expect, the social and environmental implications of this are tremendous.

First, there are the issues related to the disposal of fast fashion. Being made from lower-quality fabrics, the clothes are not designed to last and generally do not withstand more than a season or two before they are relegated either to the back of the wardrobe or to the scrap heap. In the past, most donations of used clothes have been from developed countries to developing countries. However, with the availability of cheap clothes now increasing in all countries, including in developing countries, the demand for used clothes has fallen significantly. This means that, in many cases, discarded clothes now go to landfill. For communities living nearby, the impacts are insidious and unsightly, encroaching as they do on the towns and fields located close by.

Second, there are various human rights issues relating to the production of fast fashion. These take a range of forms and occur at different stages of the apparel supply chain. Forced and child labour have been reported in some labour-intensive parts of the supply chain, such as the cotton-picking industry in Uzbekistan, and in the spinning and weaving stages of the chain. Further along the supply chain, child labour is also prevalent among home-based and pieceworkers of textiles. Given the nature of this work away from the factory and public arena, in many countries it is very difficult to regulate and enforce domestic and international laws prohibiting child labour.

Given the highly feminised nature of the apparel workforce, as mentioned above, it is unsurprising that women are disproportionately affected by the industry's adverse impacts on human rights. More than 80 per cent of workers in the apparel industry in Asia are young women, largely from poor, rural backgrounds. Women are particularly vulnerable to exploitation, as they are exposed to high levels of abuse and are often paid 10 to 30 per cent less than men for work of equal value.[2] For example, a 2016 Human Rights Watch Report found that many women workers in the apparel industry experience sexual abuse, harassment, and discrimination. In addition, the right to maternity leave is often not granted to workers.

For all workers, reasonable working hours and safe working conditions appear to be ongoing challenges. The industry is one of the most labour-intensive in the world and, in many instances, workers are expected to work unreasonably long hours in enclosed spaces and unsafe conditions. In Bangladesh, for example, many apparel workers work 14- to 16-hour days (often for six days per week).

Another significant issue is the underpayment of workers and their inability to access a living wage. Notably, the minimum monthly wage for garment workers in India is US$65;[3] in Bangladesh it is US$71,[4] and US$297 in Shanghai.[5] These rates contrast starkly to the wages of retailers and apparel company executives in this multi-billion-dollar industry.

Example: Rana Plaza

Safe working conditions in the apparel industry were brought to the world's attention after the 2013 Rana Plaza factory collapse in Bangladesh in which 1,134 workers were killed and another 2,500 workers were injured.[6] The clothing produced at Rana Plaza supplied numerous international clothing brands.

In response to the 2013 Rana Plaza collapse, several significant initiatives have emerged in the apparel industry.

First, more than 200 companies voluntarily signed an Accord on Fire and Building Safety in Bangladesh ("the Accord"). This is a five-year, independent, legally binding agreement between global brands, retailers, and trade unions designed to build a safe and healthy Bangladeshi ready-made garment industry. It includes factory inspections and safety training. Following the expiration of the 2013 Accord, the 2018 Accord is now open for signature.[7]

Second, owing to concerns regarding exposure after signing the Accord, 28 North American entities voluntarily signed a similar, but less stringent, Alliance for Bangladesh Worker Safety ("the Alliance"). Similarly, this is a legally binding, five-year commitment to improve safety in Bangladeshi garment factories. The Alliance's website states that: "the Alliance will join with credible, local partners in the weeks ahead to form a joint entity that will continue to oversee inspections, monitoring, worker training and helpline services over the long term."[8]

Third, the International Labour Organization set up the Rana Plaza Donors Trust Fund. This fund consolidates voluntary donations by businesses and the public to provide compensation to those affected by the Rana Plaza collapse.

While human rights violations persist in many apparel companies' supply chains, these initiatives demonstrate that some progress in the industry is being made.

Other notable initiatives

In addition to membership of the multi-stakeholder initiatives noted above, there are other innovative ways that some fashion retailers are seeking to limit their adverse impacts on people and the environment.

Various fashion brands have introduced recycling initiatives. For example, H&M's garment collecting initiative encourages people to drop off their textiles in any H&M store – "no matter brand or condition" – and clothes will either be reworn (sold as second-hand), reused (turning them into other products like cleaning cloths), or recycled (turning them into textile fibres and used in products like insulation). Likewise, Zara and Nike have collection facilities for old garments and shoes, respectively.

Other initiatives, emerging out of the sharing economy, are high-end monthly rental services pioneered by Rent the Runway and others, like Le Tote and Style Lend. In the case of Rent the Runway, members pay a monthly fee in exchange for access to a selection of the latest top designers' pieces delivered to their door.[9]

Among the service's benefits, the company pitches to prospective members that they will "feel put together always," and that they can "influence the future." In relation to the latter, they exhort members to: "Power the sharing economy and divert unnecessary waste from landfills. Rent, reduce, reuse." However, given the frequent shipping and dry cleaning required by these services, it is questionable what their environmental benefits (if any) will be. However, from the perspective of mitigating the human rights impacts of the fast fashion industry, they are likely to have a positive impact.

Notes

1 Clean Clothes Campaign, *Facts on the Global Garment Industry*: https://cleanclothes.org/resources/publications/factsheets/general-factsheet-garment-industry-february-2015.pdf.
2 For further information, see: Oxfam Australia, *Still in the Dark Report: Lifting the Cloak on the Global Garment Trade* (2016):

www.oxfam.org.au/wp-content/uploads/2016/04/Labour-Rights-Still-in-the-Dark-Report.pdf; Baptist World Aid Australia, *The 2016 Australian Fashion Report: The Truth Behind the Barcode* (2016): www.baptistworldaid.org.au/assets/Be-Fair-Section/FashionReport.pdf; CORE, *Beyond Compliance: Effective Reporting under the Modern Slavery Act* (2016): http://corporate-responsibility.org/wp-content/uploads/2016/03/CSO_TISC_guidance_final_digitalversion_16.03.16.pdf.

3 Clean Clothes Campaign, *Facts on India's Garment Industry*: https://cleanclothes.org/resources/publications/factsheets/india-factsheet-february-2015.pdf.

4 Baptist World Aid Australia, *The 2016 Australian Fashion Report: The Truth Behind the Barcode* (2016): www.baptistworldaid.org.au/assets/Be-Fair-Section/FashionReport.pdf.

5 International Labour Organization, *Minimum Wages in the Global Garment Industry: Update for 2015* (2015): www.ilo.org/asia/what-wedo/publications/WCMS_436867/lang-en/index.htm.

6 Bdnews24.com, *Cases over Rana Plaza Collapse See Little Progress in Three Years* (23 April 2016): http://bdnews24.com/bangladesh/2016/04/23/cases-over-rana-plaza-collapse-see-little-progress-in-three-years.

7 Accord on Fire and Building Safety in Bangladesh, 2018. Accessed on 20 June 2018: http://bangladeshaccord.org/wp-content/uploads/2018-Accord-full-text.pdf.

8 Alliance for Bangladesh Worker Safety, Statement on the Fifth Anniversary of the Rana Plaza Collapse. Accessed on 20 June 2018: www.bangladeshworkersafety.org/478-rana-plaza-statement-yr5.

9 See Rent the Runway website. Accessed on 30 July 2018: www.renttherunway.com.

Chapter 16

Fast-moving consumer goods industry

Overview

Fast-moving consumer goods ("FMCG") or consumer packaged goods are products that are sold quickly and at a relatively low cost, such as soft drinks, chocolate bars, bags of rice and tinned goods. Generally, the profit margin on FMCGs is small. However, when high volumes are sold, they generate substantial profits.

FMCG supply chains are particularly complex. Before a product reaches the supermarket or grocery shelf, primary producers, sub-contractors, manufacturers, and distributors – often operating across multiple countries – are involved in the supply chain. When the variety of product lines available in a supermarket are considered, the tentacles of their diverse and multiple supply chains are extremely unwieldly and difficult to monitor. Given this, conducting human rights due diligence and preventing and addressing human rights violations are especially complicated.

In addition to these supply chain challenges, supermarkets are under increasing pressure to deliver more for customers for less. They face growing competition not only from other supermarkets but also from industry disruptors such as meal delivery service operators, which remove any need for customers to even visit a supermarket (either in person or online). In such a competitive and cost-conscious climate, where the demand for ever-increasing efficiencies and savings is unrelenting, the potential implications for labour standards and human rights are significant.

Example: Thailand's fishing industry

These tensions and challenges have come into sharp focus in the context of abuses occurring in Thailand's multibillion-dollar fishing industry.

Recent investigations have revealed people trafficking, slavery, forced labour, and other human rights violations on fishing boats and in Thai processing facilities. Seafood from the boats and factories affected have been traced to supermarkets in the United States, Europe, and Australia.

Human Rights Watch's 2018 Report, *Hidden Chains: Rights Abuses and Forced Labor in Thailand's Fishing Industry*, paints a stark picture.[1] Some examples of abuse from the report include:

- beatings, violence, and murder of workers by skippers seeking to maintain control over their crews through fear and intimidation;
- failure to ensure the health, safety, and welfare of workers, resulting in serious work-related injuries, including the loss of limbs, disability, and death, without any action taken by the employer to either prevent or remediate the causes;
- crews forced to work around the clock on shifts of up to 18 to 24 hours (sometimes for multiple days on end), with inadequate rest or sleep;
- debt bondage – that is, fishers trapped by employers who confiscate their registration cards and tell them they are unable to leave until they pay off significant debts incurred in their recruitment and transport to Thailand; and
- exploitative payment systems – including the underpayment of workers, payment only for time at sea (not in port), and fraudulent deductions from workers' salaries for the value of the catch, goods, or services.

Likewise, earlier investigations by the Associated Press (in 2015) and the *Guardian* (in 2014) revealed egregious human rights violations including beatings, forced labour, torture, and the murder of workers on Thai fishing boats.

Further, in June 2016, a civil lawsuit was filed in the United States, accusing four US firms and Thailand of violating the US *Trafficking Victims Protection Reauthorization Act 2013*.

Actions taken and lessons learned

In response to the exposés mentioned above, the Thai Government has overhauled its fishing industry's monitoring, control, and management regimes. This has included the introduction of more stringent inspections of boats every time they arrive and depart a port, and stronger laws and penalties for violating fishers' rights.

As part of strengthening law enforcement, the Thai Government has established a special working team to speed up investigations into alleged offences.

A press release from the Ministry of Foreign Affairs of the Kingdom of Thailand, issued in response to the Human Rights Watch report, states: "As a result of the [*sic*] efforts, the overall situation of workers in the fisheries sector of Thailand over the past 3 years has drastically improved."[2]

Nevertheless, Human Rights Watch questions the efficacy of these measures. The report states: "The absence of legal provisions treating forced labor as a stand-alone offense obstructs Thai government efforts to identify and assist individuals in situations facing severe rights abuses that are not a direct consequence of trafficking in persons."[3]

Also, it underlines the unintended adverse implications of the Government's introduction of a pink card registration system for those working in the fishing industry. The policy objectives behind the pink card system were to register undocumented migrants, facilitate labour inspections in port and at sea, and enable the portability of pink cards when fishers change employers.

However, in practice, the registration system appears to have restricted workers' freedom of movement and, in doing so, placed them in an even more vulnerable position to forced labour. Pink card holders need their employer's and provincial authority's approval to travel outside their province of registration, and their legal status is tied to a specific employer or employers.[4] Given the high degree of labour mobility intrinsic to the fishing industry, Human Rights Watch argues that migrant worker registration policies should not obstruct workers' freedom to change employers.

To address the egregious abuses in the Thai fishing industry, attempts have been made to launch class action law suits in the United States against companies that have imported seafood from Thai suppliers connected with human rights abuses. Plaintiffs claimed that companies were breaching consumer protection statutes by failing to disclose that the goods were the product of slave labour.

Companies can increase visibility over their supply chains by forming coalitions with non-governmental organisations. For example, Project Issara is a public–private alliance established in Thailand in January 2014 which focuses its attention on human trafficking in South East Asia, including in the seafood industry.[5] Project Issara has formed a coalition of ten United Kingdom supermarket companies and seafood importers to address trafficking and forced labour. It requires businesses to disclose their seafood supply chain information and encourages suppliers to cooperate with the Project on monitoring.

Another example of a proactive approach is the 2015 Verité Report commissioned by Nestlé to better understand the risks of human rights abuses in its Thai shrimp supply chain.[6] Following a three-month assessment, Verité reported indicators of forced labour, trafficking, and child labour among sea-based and land-based workers engaged in the production sites covered by the assessment.[7]

In response, Nestlé has produced an action plan for the responsible sourcing of seafood, which includes incorporating new tracing requirements into commercial relationships, implementing training programmes for boat owners and captains, and publicly reporting on progress, challenges, and failures.

As the examples above demonstrate, merely having visibility over a direct supplier is likely to be insufficient given the complexity and dynamism of many FMCG supply chains. Instead, it is critical that companies conduct ongoing human rights due diligence throughout their supply chains to ensure that they identify potential adverse impacts on human rights with which they may be involved. Once these risks are identified, the company must be proactive in responding to prevent, avoid, or mitigate them.

Notes

1 Human Rights Watch, *Hidden Chains: Rights Abuses and Forced Labor in Thailand's Fishing Industry*, 2018. Accessed on 4 July 2018: www.hrw.org/report/2018/01/23/hidden-chains/rights-abuses-and-forced-labor-thailands-fishing-industry.

2 Ministry of Foreign Affairs of the Kingdom of Thailand, Press Release, 27 April 2018. Accessed on 4 July 2018: www.mfa.go.th/main/en/news3/6886/88578-Thailand%E2%80%99s-Response-to-the-Comments-of-Human-Right.html.

3 Human Rights Watch, *Hidden Chains: Rights Abuses and Forced Labor in Thailand's Fishing Industry*, 2018, Conclusion.

4 As above.

5 Project Issara, Our Story. Accessed on 4 July 2018: www.issara institute.org/about-issara.

6 *A Verite Assessment of Recruitment Practices and Migrant Labor Conditions in Nestle's Thai Shrimp Supply Chain: An Examination of Forced Labor and Other Human Rights Risks Endemic to the Thai Seafood Sector*, 2016. Accessed on 4 July 2018: www.verite.org/wp-content/uploads/2016/11/NestleReport-ThaiShrimp_prepared-by-Verite.pdf.

7 As above, "B.Key Findings," p. 1.

Chapter 17

Electronics industry

Overview: conflict minerals in the electronics industry

As supply chains go increasingly global, we rarely stop to consider the human costs of producing advanced electronic devices – like smartphones, tablets, and laptops. Yet, human rights challenges are particularly pertinent to the industry given its reliance on so-called "conflict minerals" to make capacitors for electronic goods.

Conflict minerals are tantalum, tin, tungsten, and gold (often referred to as "3TG") when sourced from the Democratic Republic of the Congo ("DRC"). While these minerals are also sourced from various other countries around the world, when derived from mines in the DRC they have been associated with the decades-long civil war there in which more than 5.4 million people have died.

The civil war in the DRC has been funded, in large part, by rebel and government-backed militias. The militias often control the country's mineral deposits – either directly or indirectly (through taxing and exploiting artisanal miners and local populations). Egregious human rights violations have been connected to the militias' activities. These include: murder, mass rape as a weapon of war, torture, forced labour, and the conscription of child soldiers. Accordingly, electronics companies purchasing conflict minerals from the DRC have been implicated in the gross human rights violations occurring there.[1]

Several characteristics of electronics supply chains heighten the risks of human rights violations occurring in them. These include: their complex and dispersed nature, the absence of legal protections for human rights and labour standards in many of the countries which the supply chains pass through, and the nature and location of the work (that is, 3TG minerals are often sourced from remote, artisanal mines in the DRC).[2]

Human rights violations in eastern DRC

In 2015, the United Nations Group of Experts published its Final Report on the DRC.[3] It found that, despite some advances to validate minerals as "conflict free" and to improve adherence to international human rights standards, armed groups continued to control many mining sites and profit from the minerals trade in eastern DRC and neighbouring countries.

The Final Report found that tantalum (along with tin and tungsten) continues to be smuggled from eastern DRC through neighbouring countries, undermining confidence in international certification and traceability mechanisms.

Baudouin K. Hamuli, the National Coordinator for the International Conference on the Great Lakes Region (ICGLR), also chairs the committee of national experts that advises the government on peace in eastern DRC. He stated: "Coltan is part of the economy of war in Eastern DRC. The way coltan has been exploited to date shows very little respect for human rights."[4]

Of the five million people who have died in recent conflicts in eastern DRC, it is estimated that around 40 per cent were women and children. Recruitment of children as soldiers has been endemic, along with widespread sexual violence against women as a weapon of war. The warfare is complex and ever-changing, with an intricate web of rebel and government-backed militias in combat with each other.

To a large extent, the DRC operates as a law-free zone, in which the Congolese National Army ("FARDC") and various rebel groups have seized control of lucrative 3TG mines. Militia groups commit a range of human rights violations. These include exposing miners to dangerous working conditions, demanding excessive working hours, and exploiting child labour. The control of mining operations, in turn, finances the ongoing armed conflict, with the FARDC reportedly sometimes collecting more than US$100,000 a month through the imposition of illegal tariffs on miners.

Actions taken and lessons learned

The United States Congress has recognised that the "exploitation and trade of conflict minerals originating in the [DRC] is helping to finance conflict characterized by extreme levels of violence in the Eastern [DRC], particularly sexual and gender-based violence."[5]

In 2010, in an attempt to address these severe human rights violations, Congress enacted Section 1502 of the *Dodd–Frank Wall Street Reform and Consumer Protection Act* ("Dodd–Frank Act"). It requires regulated entities to disclose to the US Securities and Exchange Commission ("SEC") whether any of their products contain conflict minerals originating from the DRC.

Where products do contain DRC conflict minerals, public companies must submit a report to the SEC disclosing the source and chain of custody of the minerals (the Dodd–Frank Act defines conflict minerals as the ores columbite-tantalite (coltan), cassiterite, and wolframite from which, respectively, tantalum, tin, and tungsten are derived. Gold is also defined as a conflict mineral).

In its 2016 *ICT Benchmark Findings Report*, Know the Chain reported that 16 out of the 20 information and communications technology companies assessed had a process in place to trace conflict minerals entering their supply chains beyond their first tier suppliers.[6] It appears that these efforts have been largely driven by the disclosure regulations in the Dodd–Frank Act.

In the DRC, it seems that the Dodd–Frank provisions have also spurred some progress. Civil society groups in the DRC are more active in advocating responsible mining and there is improved monitoring of mines and increased awareness among miners of their rights.

In another positive development, some companies that are not subject to the Dodd–Frank provisions (including Panasonic and Samsung) have followed their US competitors and now publish information on their supply chain due diligence on their websites. Likewise, the Taiwanese computer company Acer has chosen to annually publish its own version of a conflict minerals report.[7]

However, despite these achievements, it seems that serious issues remain. Global Witness reported a "crisis of confidence" following the introduction of the Dodd–Frank Act. Contrary to the law's intention, several companies reacted to it by encouraging their suppliers to leave the DRC altogether, rather than stay and comply with the enhanced requirements for responsible mining. Global Witness states: "This impacted mineral exports from Congo's North and South Kivu provinces from 2011 onwards, affecting the livelihoods of thousands of artisanal miners in eastern Congo."[8]

In addition, the Trump administration has announced that it is reconsidering the conflict minerals law. This follows a US Court of Appeals Decision in which the Court found that aspects of the law violate the First Amendment of the Constitution by requiring regulated entities to report to the SEC and state on their websites that any of their products have "not been found to be 'DRC conflict free'."[9] In a statement released in April 2017, the SEC stated that, given the current uncertainty about the conflict minerals provisions, the SEC will not recommend enforcement actions against companies failing to meet their disclosure requirements under the law.[10]

These developments are particularly concerning. Reports indicate that, despite some progress having been made, egregious human rights violations are ongoing in the DRC and the minerals trade continues to finance war there.

Nevertheless, on a more positive note, the responses of major companies to the possible executive action by the US Government has been more encouraging. In its letter to the Acting SEC Chairman (dated March 2017), Global Witness affirms:

Intel and Apple both expressed a commitment to compliance with the Rule because they "believe in doing the right thing." The jewelry company Richline added that "the cause is worthy of these efforts." Tiffany & Co. emphasized that "while we intend to maintain the guiding principles of our Conflict Minerals Policy regardless of regulation, we firmly believe that the continued existence of Federal regulation that addresses the sourcing of conflict minerals provides an important framework for industry, laying the foundation for protection of human rights and responsible sourcing efforts in Congo and beyond."[11]

We can only hope that the leadership on conflict minerals demonstrated by these corporations (and others) will be matched by the political leaders tasked with determining the future direction of this complex and important legislative and policy area.

Notes

1 For more information, see Newton, Alex and Soundar, Jude. "Blood in your mobile: Implications for the electronics industry of human rights violations in the Democratic Republic of the Congo." *Ethical Corporation Magazine*, 14 August 2014.
2 Artisanal mining is small-scale and informal mining often conducted by individuals or small teams. It generally utilises primitive tools to clear some jungle, dig into the soil, and extract whatever minerals are close to the surface. Through an informal market, minerals are then sold on to middlemen and make their way to buyers along precarious, and often illegal, routes.
3 UN Security Council, *Final Report of the Group of Experts on the Democratic Republic of the Congo*, S/2015/19, 12 January 2015. Accessed on 5 July 2018: www.securitycouncilreport.org/atf/cf/%7b 65BFCF9B-6D27-4E9C-8CD3-CF6E4FF96FF9%7d/s_2015_19.pdf.
4 Newton, Alex and Soundar, Jude, note 1.
5 *Dodd–Frank Wall Street Reform and Consumer Protection Act 2010* (US), p. 838.
6 Know the Chain, *ICT Benchmark Findings Report*, June 2016. Accessed on 5 July 2018: https://knowthechain.org/wp-content/ uploads/2016/06/KTC_ICT-External-Report_Web_21June2016FINAL _Small.pdf.

7 Global Witness, Letter to Michael S. Piwowar, Acting Chairman United States Securities and Exchange Commission, 17 March 2017, p. 5. Accessed on 5 July 2018: www.sec.gov/comments/statement-013117/cll2-1648467-148482.pdf.

8 Global Witness, *Briefing: US Conflict Minerals Law*, 15 November 2017. Accessed on 5 July 2018: www.globalwitness.org/en/campaigns/conflict-minerals/dodd-frank-act-section-1502.

9 *Nat'l Ass'n of Mfrs., et al.* v. *SEC*, 800 F.3d 518, 530 (D.C. Cir 2015).

10 US Securities and Exchange Commission, Updated Statement on the Effect of the Court of Appeals Decision on the Conflict Minerals Rule, 7 April 2017. Accessed on 6 July 2018: www.sec.gov/news/public-statement/corpfin-updated-statement-court-decision-conflict-minerals-rule.

11 Global Witness, Letter to Michael S. Piwowar, Acting Chairman United States Securities and Exchange Commission, 17 March 2017, p. 2. Accessed on 6 July 2018: www.sec.gov/comments/statement-013117/cll2-1648467-148482.pdf.

Chapter 18

Banking and finance industry

Overview

Following the global financial crisis of 2007/2008, the spotlight of global scrutiny has shone more brightly on the banking and finance sector.

Around the world, a spate of scandals has implicated some of the largest banks and financial institutions. The examples are plentiful. A few of the most notorious include:

- In September 2008, Lehman Brothers (then the fourth-largest investment bank in the United States) filed for bankruptcy, disclosing its losses of US$3.9 billion. The collapse was blamed on Lehman Brothers' over-exposure to the subprime mortgage market, which it had pursued aggressively over the course of the previous decade.[1]
- In 2012, HSBC was found guilty of (and admitted to) laundering hundreds of millions of dollars for the Mexican narcotics syndicate led by "El Chapo" Guzman. The drug trade has resulted in more than 100,000 deaths and many thousands more missing.
- In 2015, a whistle-blower leaked 11.5 million documents to the German newspaper *Süddeutsche Zeitung*, providing details of offshore entities allegedly set up by a Panama law firm, Mossack Fonseca, to help its wealthy clients evade taxes and international sanctions. The documents linked

financial institutions in Canada, Denmark, France, Germany, Spain, Sweden, and Switzerland to money laundering through over 1,200 offshore companies.[2]

However, one issue that seems to have flown largely under the radar (both publicly and from the perspective of the banks themselves) is the banks' capacity to impact adversely on human rights. There are numerous ways banks have the potential to impact detrimentally on human rights. A few are outlined below.

Impacts through banks' own activities

The first way is perhaps the most obvious: human rights impacts through banks' own activities.

Banks' activities invariably impact a wide range of people: their customers, employees or prospective employees, and the community more broadly. As an example, Australia's 2018 Royal Commission into Misconduct in the Banking, Super-annuation and Financial Services Industry has uncovered various ways in which banks have targeted vulnerable people (including Indigenous people and farmers), sometimes with devastating effects on people's lives.

The ANZ Bank is accused of failing to promote its non-fee, basic access account, instead pushing Aboriginal customers to more complex and expensive products, such as overdraft accounts. These accounts allow customers to withdraw more money than they have in their account and, accordingly, incur a penalty interest rate of around 17 per cent.[3]

Likewise, the Royal Commission has heard that the National Australia Bank used default interest payments as a "strategic tool" to apply pressure to farmers suffering from the effects of natural disasters (such as floods and drought).[4] In several cases, banks appear to have overseen conflicts of interest between their internal appraisals of property prices and their sales-driven culture, which incentivised profits to the detriment of their responsible lending obligations.

In addition, allegations of gender discrimination and sexual harassment have also embroiled some of the major banks in recent years. As outlined in Chapter 9, the investment bank Goldman Sachs is engaged in long-running legal proceedings brought by former employees alleging widespread gender discrimination by the bank on a range of grounds.[5]

Impacts linked to banks' operations, products or services

A second area of risk is human rights impacts directly linked to banks' operations, products, or services through their business relationships. In particular, corporate loans and project finance are areas where a bank may be directly linked to an adverse impact through a business relationship. Oxfam's 2014 Report, *Banking on Shaky Ground*, revealed connections between the four major Australian Banks (Commonwealth Bank of Australia, ANZ, National Australia Bank, and Westpac) and allegations of land grabbing overseas by the banks' clients.[6]

Land grabs are large-scale land acquisitions that violate human rights; flout the principle of free, prior, and informed consent; or take place without, or disregard, a thorough assessment of social, economic, and environmental impacts.

In its follow-up report released in 2016, *Still Banking on Land Grabs*, Oxfam found that progress since its 2014 report had been minimal. It stated: "While NAB and Westpac appear to be taking their exposure to land grabbing as a serious risk to their businesses, each developing new policies on land-related issues, CBA and ANZ have done little."[7]

In addition, in October 2014 a specific instance complaint under the OECD Guidelines for Multinational Enterprises was made against ANZ to the Australian National Contact Point for the Guidelines ("ANCP"), located in the Treasury.[8] The complaint related to ANZ's part-financing from 2011 to 2014 to a developer of a Cambodian sugar plantation, Phnom Penh Sugar ("PPS"), that was linked to child labour, military-backed land grabs, destruction of crops and property, forced evictions, and food shortages. PPS also allegedly participated in the arbitrary arrests and intimidation of villagers, and dangerous working conditions that have resulted in the deaths of several workers. In July 2014, ANZ severed its ties with PPS after PPS suddenly repaid its entire loan.

In her Final Statement closing the case, published in June 2018, the ANCP stated:

> in this case it is difficult to reconcile ANZ's decision to take on PPS as a client with its own internal policies and procedures – which appear to accord with the OECD Guidelines – as the potential risks associated with this decision would likely have been readily apparent.[9]

The ANCP recommended that ANZ instigate methods to promote and demonstrate internal compliance with its own stated corporate standards with respect to human rights; that it strengthen its due diligence arrangements to ensure they are adequate to manage the risks connected to its lending activities; and that it establish a grievance resolution mechanism supporting the effective operation of its standards in relation to human rights.[10]

Impacts through banks' investments

A third way banks can adversely impact human rights is through their investments, especially in companies and/or regions with poor human rights records. For example, a 2013 complaint under the OECD Guidelines against the South Korean iron and steel company POSCO also implicated two of its investors: the Norwegian Bank Investment Management ("NBIM") and the Dutch pension Fund ABP and its pension administrator.[11]

The complaint concerned NBIM's investments in POSCO, a company responsible for various human rights violations at a proposed iron mine, steel plant, and associated infrastructure in the state of Odisha, India.

Parallel complaints were considered by the Dutch and Norwegian National Contact Points. Both issued final statements indicating that, under the OECD Guidelines, companies (including banks) have a responsibility to undertake human rights due diligence – and to engage with the company in which they are invested – whether they are a minority or a majority investor. That is, it is no excuse for a bank to claim it is only a minority investor in a company adversely impacting human rights.

Actions taken and notable initiatives

There are a range of multi-stakeholder initiatives specifically addressing the banking and finance sector. These include the Equator Principles, the IFC Performance Standards on Environmental and Social Sustainability, and the OECD Common Approaches for OECD Export Credit Agencies.

In addition, in 2011 the Thun Group was formed as an informal group of bank representatives working together to advance understanding of the UN Guiding Principles in the banking context, and to consider how they apply across a range of different banking activities. Its members include UBS, Credit Suisse, Barclays, BBVA, BNP Paribas, Deutsche Bank, ING, RBS, Standard Chartered, UniCredit, and JP Morgan. The Group meets regularly and is convened by UBS. As of July 2018, the Thun Group had issued two discussion papers: in 2013 and 2017.[12]

The Thun Group's 2017 discussion paper is particularly notable for the significant consternation and criticism it generated among many experts and stakeholders in the business and human rights field. Contrary to the UN Guiding Principles, the 2017 paper assumes that banks generally do *not cause or contribute to human rights impacts* by providing finance to a client, and therefore are not responsible for remediating these impacts. Instead, the paper attempts to limit banks' responsibility for human rights impacts to situations where there is a significant, direct transactional link with clients whose actions are affecting human rights impacts.[13]

Professor David Kinley of Sydney University (among many others) has criticised the Thun Group for what he considers its "strict transactional approach" to the issue of human rights.[14] He underlines the Thun Group's restrictive approach to interpreting banks' responsibilities, even when they are directly linked to human rights impacts. For example, the responsibility to prevent and mitigate adverse impacts on human rights is discretionary under the Guiding Principles in the case of a business that is directly linked through its business relationships to adverse impacts (unlike businesses causing or contributing to those impacts).[15] Nevertheless, Kinley is right to question the genuineness of the whole Thun Group enterprise when it appears to advocate a minimalist response to banks' human rights responsibilities.

These question marks are only multiplied by both papers' lengthy closing disclaimers, which seek to absolve any financial institution from any legal obligations arising from the discussion papers. Kinley says: "How a 'discussion paper' could deliver any such evidently dreaded outcomes is a mystery. What, alas, is not is the Thun Group's palpable anxiety that banks might be required to walk as they talk."[16]

In an open letter, BankTrack, other NGO representatives, and academics challenged many of the assertions made by the Thun Group in its 2017 discussion paper.[17] The BankTrack authors note the UN's advice that banks may indeed *contribute* to human rights abuses through their finance. They also clarify the meaning of *directly linked* in the context of the banking and finance sector, drawing on advice provided by the UN Office of the High Commissioner for Human Rights ("UN OHCHR") to the OECD Working Party. They state that the UN OHCHR:

> gives examples of circumstances where financial institutions *may contribute, be directly linked* or have no link to a human rights impact via their finance. It advises that financing can contribute to a human rights impact, "such as if financing is provided for a project that will result in widespread displacement of communities, without safeguards in place". Banks would then have a responsibility to remedy such a human rights impact [emphasis added].[18]

The UN Working Group on Business and Human Rights[19] and Professor Ruggie also responded to the Thun Group's 2017 discussion paper, expressing their significant concerns.[20]

Professor Ruggie professed that he is "deeply troubled" by the discussion paper, which "misconstrues *the* central Guiding Principle regarding the corporate responsibility to respect human rights (UNGP 13)" (emphasis in the original).[21] Further, Ruggie stated that "several of the hypothetical cases could fall into the 'contribute to' harm category ... depending on additional situational factors."[22] Instead, the Thun paper classified these cases as examples of mere "linkage."

Following the Thun Group's paper, the UN OHCHR produced detailed guidance for the banking sector: *OHCHR Response to Request from BankTrack for Advice Regarding the Application of the UN Guiding Principles on Business and Human Rights in the Context of the Banking Sector*. The guidance discusses the factors that may be used to determine whether a bank is causing or contributing to, or has a direct link to, an adverse impact arising from its finance.[23]

It is regrettable that the Thun Group's recent work has generated such a maelstrom of confusion and controversy. While some updates were made to its discussion paper following the avalanche of negative feedback received (as outlined above), the central concern – the assertion that banks do not generally contribute to human rights abuses through their finance – remains.[24] Ironically, as BankTrack has observed, the responses to the Thun Group's paper have proved to be more influential than the paper itself.[25]

As this chapter has outlined, banks can be involved in adverse impacts on human rights in a range of ways. It is crucial that bankers and their advisors engage proactively and meaningfully with these issues, and with other stakeholders and experts in the business and human rights field to better understand their responsibilities. The banking and finance sector can also look to the examples provided by other sectors (as outlined in the preceding chapters) to see the real benefits of leadership, and of adopting a more expansive and positive approach to defining their responsibilities.

Notes

1 RepRisk. "RepRisk Report 2006–2016: Ten years of global banking scandals," 2017, p. 2. Accessed on 8 July 2018: www.reprisk. com/content/5-publications/1-special-reports/51-ten-years-of-global-banking-scandals/repriskreport-banking.pdf.

2 RepRisk, as above, p. 6.

3 ABC News. "Banking royal commission: ANZ's treatment of Indigenous people may have broken law," 6 July 2018. Accessed on 9 July 2018: www.abc.net.au/news/2018–07–06/funeral-insurance-suppliers-to-indigenous-communities-face-char/9950944.

4 ABC News. "Banking royal commission: Lenders accused of misconduct over treatment of farmers," 6 July 2018. Accessed on 9 July 2018: www.abc.net.au/news/2018-07-06/banking-royal-commission-hears-farm-loan-misconduct-claims/9948010.

5 For details see Chapter 9.

6 Oxfam. *Banking on Shaky Ground: Australia's Big Four Banks and Land Grabs*, 2014. Accessed on 8 July 2018: www.oxfam.org.au/wp-content/uploads/site-media/pdf/2014-47%20australia's%20big%204%20banks%20and%20land%20grabs_fa_web.pdf.

7 Oxfam. *Still Banking on Land Grabs: Australia's big four banks and land grabs*, 2016. Accessed on 8 July 2018: https://resources.oxfam.org.au/pages/view.php?ref=1734&k=c456e625dc.

8 Specific instance complaint under OECD Guidelines for Multinational Enterprises by Inclusive Development International (IDI) and Equitable Cambodia (EC) Against Australia New Zealand Banking Group (ANZ), concerning financial services provided to Phnom Penh Sugar Company. Accessed on 9 July 2018: www.inclusivedevelopment.net/wp-content/uploads/2014/10/Specific-Instance-against-ANZ-FINAL.pdf

9 Australian National Contact Point. Final Statement. Accessed on 10 December 2018: https://cdn.tspace.gov.au/uploads/sites/112/2018/10/11_AusNCP_Final_Statement.pdf.

10 ANCP. Final Statement, Executive Summary, as above, pp. 2–3.

11 OECD Watch. "Norwegian NCP publishes final statement in POSCO/NBIM case," 27 May 2013. Accessed on 9 July 2018: www.oecdwatch.org/news-en/norwegian-ncp-publishes-final-statement-in-posco-nbim-case.

12 The Thun Group's first and second discussion papers are available online. Accessed on 10 July 2018: www.ubs.com/global/en/about_ubs/ubs-and-society/how-we-do-business/sustainability/thun-group.html.

13 Kinley, David. "Artful Dodgers: Banks and their human rights responsibilities." Sydney Law School, Legal Studies Research Paper

No. 17/17, March 2017, p. 1. Accessed on 9 July 2018: https://papers.ssrn.com/sol3/papers.cfm?abstract_id=2926215.

14 David Kinley, as above.

15 Commentary to Guiding Principle 22, p. 24 states:

> Where adverse impacts have occurred that the business enterprise has not caused or contributed to, but which are directly linked to its operations, products or services by a business relationship, the responsibility to respect human rights does not require that the enterprise itself provide for remediation, though it may take a role in doing so.

16 David Kinley, as above, p. 4, note 194.

17 Open letter to Thun Group from BankTrack and others, 14 February 2017. Accessed on 10 July 2018: www.business-humanrights.org/sites/default/files/documents/170214_Open_letter_to_Thun_Group.pdf.

18 Open letter to Thun Group from BankTrack and others, as above, p. 2.

19 Letter from Michael K. Addo, Chairperson, Working Group on the issue of human rights and transnational corporations and other business enterprises, 23 February 2017. Accessed on 10 July 2018: www.business-humanrights.org/sites/default/files/documents/20170223%20WG%20BHR%20letter%20to%20Thun%20Group.pdf.

20 Ruggie, John G. "Comments on Thun Group of Banks discussion paper on the implications of UN Guiding Principles 13 & 17 in a corporate and investment banking context," 21 February 2017. Accessed on 10 July 2018: www.business-humanrights.org/sites/default/files/documents/Thun%20Final.pdf.

21 Ruggie, John G., as above, p. 1.

22 Ruggie, John G., as above, p. 3.

23 UN OHCHR, *OHCHR Response to Request from BankTrack for Advice Regarding the Application of the UN Guiding Principles on Business and Human Rights in the Context of the Banking Sector*, 12 June 2017. Accessed on 10 July 2018: www.ohchr.org/Documents/Issues/Business/InterpretationGuidingPrinciples.pdf.

24 BankTrack. "Banks and human rights: The Thun Group must step up – BankTrack and allies urge Thun banks to make changes in new open letter," 27 March 2018. Accessed on 10 July 2018: www.banktrack.org/blog/banks_and_human_rights_the_thun_group_must_step_up#_.

25 BankTrack, as above.

Part VI

Conclusion

Conclusion

Chapter 19

Final thoughts

As the economic power of corporations has increased, so too has our awareness of their potential impacts – both positive and negative. Today, multinational corporations' supply chains wend their way in multifarious directions and combinations around the globe.

Even the production of a simple T-shirt can involve the interaction of many players along the supply chain: from the cotton growers and pickers to the spinners and weavers, to the fabric dyers and finishers, to the factory or home-based textile workers, to the distributers and retailers, and then, finally, to the shop floor – and all the other steps in between. Given this, it is understandable that many corporate executives have struggled to understand the scope (and limits) of their responsibilities for human rights.

The UN Guiding Principles have provided much-needed clarity amid the confusion. The 31 principles (and the three-tiered framework underpinning them) clearly articulate the State duty to protect human rights, the corporate responsibility to respect human rights, and the need for greater access to remedy for victims of corporate human rights abuses.

This book has tracked the social and economic background out of which the Guiding Principles emerged, and has contextualised them within broader developments in the corporate responsibility field. In doing so, we come to see the two predominant strands in corporate responsibility: one focused on business opportunity, and the other on risk. The Guiding Principles fall into the latter category: addressing the risk that companies cause, or contribute to, adverse impacts on human rights.

To properly understand the Guiding Principles, we must understand their implications for business – in both legal and non-legal terms. Human rights are first and foremost a *legal* issue for business. This is reflected by the fact that increasingly corporations face obligations under both international and domestic law.

Despite the many ongoing, and sometimes cavernous, "governance gaps" which the Guiding Principles seek to address, legislative obligations are steadily evolving and expanding in many States to recognise that corporations have responsibilities for their social and environmental impacts. Legislation combatting modern slavery in the United States, United Kingdom, and Australia, and France's duty of vigilance law are just a few examples.

Similarly, the non-legal implications for corporations failing to respect human rights can be tremendous. As various recent examples attest, a corporation causing or contributing or linked through its relationships to adverse impacts on human rights can face crippling costs both financially and in reputational terms.

Human rights are a salient risk and responsibility for all corporations to consider, regardless of their size, sector, structure, or location. It is imperative that corporate executives take proactive and ongoing measures to meet their responsibility to respect human rights. In doing so, they safeguard not only the future of their business but also the futures of the communities and individuals they interact with.

Index

Page numbers in **bold** denote tables, those in *italics* denote figures.